In der Cornelsen Lernen App findest du viele Angebote für dieses Buch.

Achte in deinem Buch auf diese Zeichen:

- Hilfe — Hole dir in der App **Hilfe** für eine Aufgabe.
- Quiz — Mache das **Quiz** in der App. Finde heraus, was du schon kannst.
- Audio 33 — Höre das **Audio** in der App.
- Video 2 — Sieh das **Video** in der App an.

1. Gib die Seitenzahl aus deinem Buch ein.

2. Du siehst die Angebote, die es zu dieser Seite gibt.

3. Wähle das Angebot, das du brauchst.

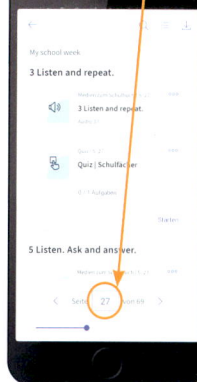

Klick!
Englisch

2

Erarbeitet von
Dr. Martina Koch
Berit Rudolph

 In der **Cornelsen Lernen App** findest du passend zu deinem Englischbuch
- Audios
- Videos
- digitale Hilfen
- interaktive Elemente

Cornelsen

Klick!
Englisch 2
Ab Jahrgangsstufe 6

Erarbeitet von
Dr. Martina Koch, Nürnberg
Berit Rudolph, Lüneburg
sowie Zoe Thorne, Haywards Heath (Songs)
und Miriam Güthler, Nürnberg (Quizzes)

In Zusammenarbeit mit der Englischredaktion
Klaus Unger; Anne Linder; Josephine Bienert-Köhler, Brianna Gorman, Chelsea Ledvinka-Heß, Denise Wendler sowie Georg Raspe, Düsseldorf (Wörterliste)

Beratende Mitwirkung
Stella Halank, Berlin; Matthias Schwarz, Mannheim; Petra Spengler, Dortmund; Gabriela Staňka, München; Amke Wolbert, Mannheim

Lizenzmanagement
Silke Kirchhoff

Layoutkonzept
Klein & Halm, Berlin

Umschlaggestaltung
Anja Rosendahl, Berlin

Layout und technische Umsetzung
Reemers Publishing Services GmbH, Krefeld

Illustrationen
Joseph Wilkins sowie Carl Pearce (Cartoons),
Beehive Illustration Agency, Cirencester, England;
Nils Fliegner, Hamburg (Umschlag)

Fotos
Anja Poehlmann, Brighton
Wir danken der Varndean School, Brighton

www.cornelsen.de

Soweit in diesem Lehrwerk Personen fotografisch abgebildet sind und ihnen von der Redaktion fiktive Namen, Berufe, Dialoge und Ähnliches zugeordnet oder diese Personen in bestimmte Kontexte gesetzt werden, dienen diese Zuordnungen und Darstellungen ausschließlich der Veranschaulichung und dem besseren Verständnis des Buchinhaltes.

Die enthaltenen Links verweisen auf digitale Inhalte, die der Verlag bei verlagsseitigen Angeboten in eigener Verantwortung zur Verfügung stellt. Links auf Angebote Dritter wurden nach den gleichen Qualitätskriterien wie die verlagsseitigen Angebote ausgewählt und bei Erstellung des Lernmittels sorgfältig geprüft. Für spätere Änderungen der verknüpften Inhalte kann keine Verantwortung übernommen werden.

Die Cornelsen Lernen App ist eine fakultative Ergänzung zu Klick!. Sie unterliegt nicht der Genehmigungspflicht.

Dieses Werk berücksichtigt die Regeln der reformierten Rechtschreibung und Zeichensetzung.

1. Auflage, 2. Druck 2026

Alle Drucke dieser Auflage sind inhaltlich unverändert und können im Unterricht nebeneinander verwendet werden.

© 2024 Cornelsen Verlag GmbH, Mecklenburgische Str. 53, 14197 Berlin, E-Mail: service@cornelsen.de

Das Werk und seine Teile sind urheberrechtlich geschützt. Jede Nutzung in anderen als den gesetzlich zugelassenen Fällen bedarf der vorherigen schriftlichen Einwilligung des Verlages. Hinweis zu §§ 60 a, 60 b UrhG: Weder das Werk noch seine Teile dürfen ohne eine solche Einwilligung an Schulen oder in Unterrichts- und Lehrmedien (§ 60 b Abs. 3 UrhG) vervielfältigt, insbesondere kopiert oder eingescannt, verbreitet oder in ein Netzwerk eingestellt oder sonst öffentlich zugänglich gemacht oder wiedergegeben werden. Dies gilt auch für Intranets von Schulen und anderen Bildungseinrichtungen.

Der Anbieter behält sich eine Nutzung der Inhalte für Text- und Data-Mining im Sinne § 44 b UrhG ausdrücklich vor.

Druck: Livonia Print, Riga

ISBN 978-3-0603-6662-0

PEFC zertifiziert
Dieses Produkt stammt aus nachhaltig bewirtschafteten Wäldern und kontrollierten Quellen.
www.pefc.de
PEFC/12-31-006

Inhaltsverzeichnis

Welcome back 4

A new student 10

Family and pets 18

Body 26

Friends 34

Food and drinks 42

My week 50

Shopping 58

Around the year 66

Meine Strategien: Hören, Sprechen, Lesen, Schreiben 72

Wörterliste 76

Let's talk: Classroom English 84

Numbers 85

Quellenverzeichnis 86

> Aufgaben zur Text- und Medienkompetenz befinden sich auf diesen Seiten: 14, 15, 17, 19, 22, 23, 25, 28, 30, 31, 33, 37, 38, 39, 41, 46, 47, 49, 54, 55, 57, 62, 63, 65, 66, 67, 69, 70.

Welcome back

1 a) Look and listen.

b) Look and find …
- Zane
- the teacher
- the books
- the doors
- the pencil case
- …

2 Look and listen. ▶ Audio 2

3 Now you: Ask and answer in your class.

▶ Quiz
▶ AH S. 3

4 Listen and rap along. ▶ Audio 3–4

1. Welcome, everybody! (2x)
2. How are you?
3. Hello, I'm fine.
4. Let's sit down.
5. It's English time.
6. 6, 5, 4, 3, 2, and 1
7. Ready, steady, let's have fun!
8. Welcome, everybody! (2x)

Welcome back

1 Listen and repeat.

▶ Audio 5
▶ Numbers S. 85

13 thirteen	30 thirty
14 fourteen	40 forty
15 fifteen	50 fifty
16 sixteen	60 sixty
17 seventeen	70 seventy
18 eighteen	80 eighty
19 nineteen	90 ninety

20 twenty   100 one hundred
21 twenty-one
22 twenty-...

▶ Quiz
▶ AH S. 4 Nr. 1

2 Play a game: Number bingo 13 to 30

3 Listen and find the numbers. Talk to a partner.

▶ Audio 6

Number 31 is blue.

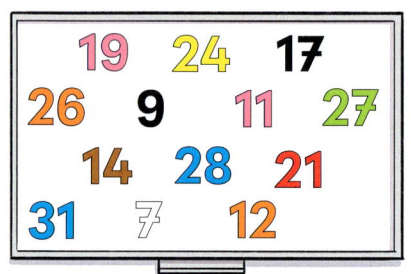

▶ Quiz
▶ AH S. 4 Nr. 2; S. 5

6   six

4 Look at the pictures. Listen and find. ▶ Audio 7

What's the right picture?

- Listen and tick.
- Be quiet, please.
- Let's do exercise 3.
- Open your books on page 35.
- Do exercise 2 for homework. ▶ Classroom English S. 84
- Say it again, please. ▶ AH S. 6

5 Cartoon: Look and listen. ▶ Audio 8

▶ AH S. 7 Nr. 4

Welcome back

1 Look and say.

What numbers can you see?

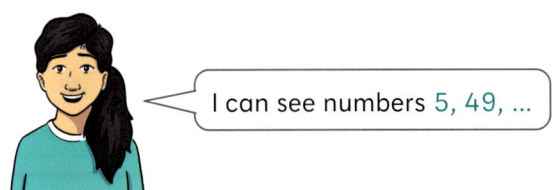

I can see numbers 5, 49, …

Five!

▶ Numbers S. 85

2 Life in Britain

Bingo ist in Großbritannien sehr beliebt. Man kann Bingo auf verschiedene Arten spielen. Ein Beispiel: Die Mitspielenden haben eine oder mehr Bingo-Karten. Eine Person zieht die Zahlen. Die Person zeigt und sagt die Zahl. Wer die Zahl auf seiner Karte hat, markiert sie. Wer zuerst eine Reihe markiert hat, ruft „Bingo!".
- Welche Spiele mit Zahlen kennst du?
- Welche Spiele spielst du besonders gerne?

▶ AH S. 7 Nr. 5

3 Listen and rap along.

▶ Audio 9–10

1 Goodbye, everybody! (2x)
2 Now the English lesson ends,
3 Let's say goodbye to our friends.
4 6, 5, 4, 3, 2, and 1
5 Ready, steady, now we're done!
7 Goodbye, everybody! (2x)

New words and phrases

👁 💬 **Look and say.**   ▶  Hilfe

13 thirteen	**20** twenty	**30** thirty
14 fourteen	**21** twenty-one	**40** forty
15 fifteen	**22** twenty-two	**50** fifty
16 sixteen	**23** twenty-three	**60** sixty
17 seventeen	**24** twenty-four	**70** seventy
18 eighteen	**25** twenty-five	**80** eighty
19 nineteen	**26** …	**90** ninety
		100 one hundred / a hundred

> Achte beim Hören und Schreiben besonders auf die Endungen:
> 14 four**teen** – 40 for**ty**   16 six**teen** – 60 six**ty**
> 15 fif**teen** – 50 fif**ty**   17 seven**teen** – …

▶ Numbers S. 85

1 page
2 exercise
3 homework

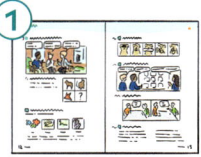  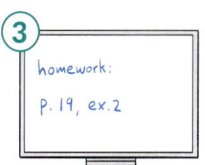

So begrüßt du jemanden nach den Ferien:

Welcome back.
Good to see you.

How are you?
– I'm fine, thanks.
– I'm OK, thanks.

> Wenn jemand zur *Begrüßung*
> *How are you?* fragt,
> antwortest du meist so:
> *I'm fine, thanks.*
> *I'm OK, thanks.*

So sagst du, wie du dich am ersten Schultag fühlst:

I'm happy to be back at school.
I'm not so happy.

So verabschiedest du dich:

Goodbye.
Bye.

▶ AH S. 8

nine 9

A new student

1 Look and say.

I can see a teacher.

There is a teacher.
There are two apples.

→
- a teacher
- an orange
- three students
- two green books
- ?

2 Look and listen.

- What is the new student's name?
- What subject is stressful for Lily?
- And you? What subject is stressful for you?

3 Listen and repeat. ▶ Audio 12

listen to a song — work with a partner — play a game — write a word

open the window — close the cupboard — go to the board — sit at the table

▶ Quiz
▶ AH S. 9

4 Play a game: Mime it!

▶ AH Bildkarten

"Play a game?" "No, that's wrong." "Write a word?" "Yes, that's right."

5 Look at the pictures. Listen and say. ▶ Audio 13

What do you do in your class?

1 We listen to songs.
2 We _____.
3 We _____.
4 We _____.

▶ AH S. 10 Nr. 1

eleven 11

A new student

1 a) Listen and repeat.  Audio 14

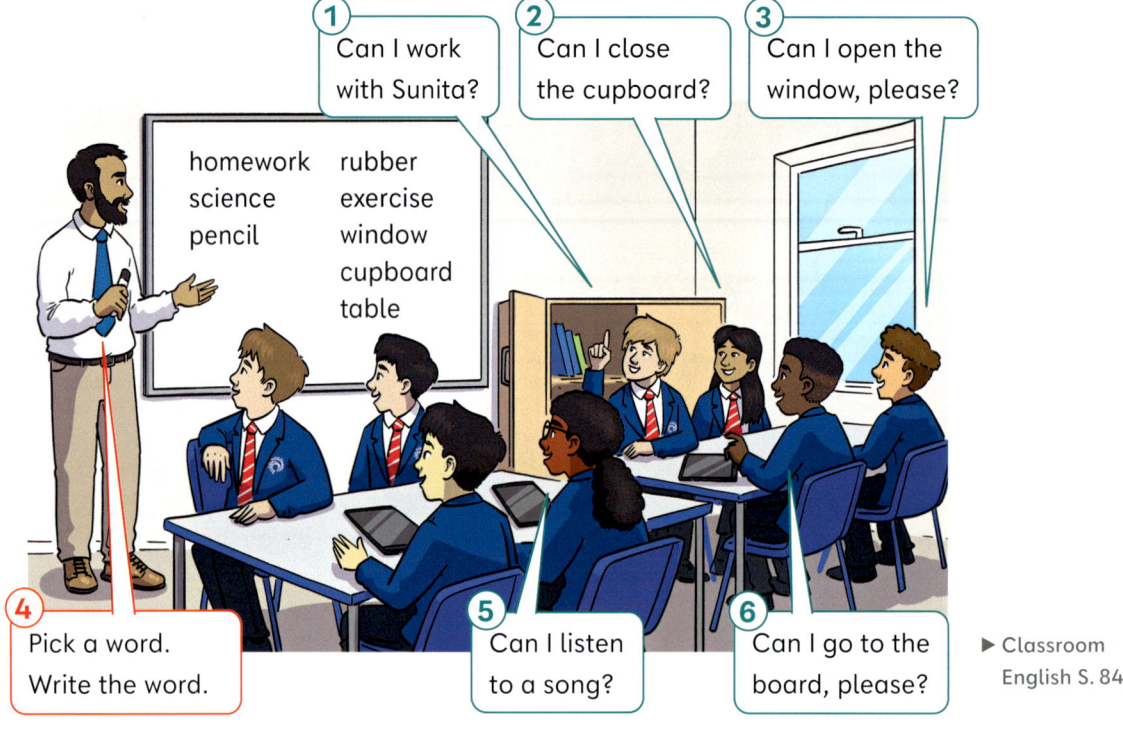

▶ Classroom English S. 84

b) Play a game: Roll the dice. Talk and write.

 Quiz

- Ich sehe mir das Wort genau an.
- Ich schreibe das Wort sorgfältig ab.
- Ich überprüfe das Wort, Buchstabe für Buchstabe.

▶ Schreib-Profi 1–3 S. 75

▶ AH S. 10 Nr. 2; S. 11

2 Listen and repeat. ▶ Audio 15

phone · in · on · under · next to

▶ Quiz

3 a) Listen to Zane, Lily, Noah and Sunita. ▶ Audio 16

b) Now you: Ask and answer.

Where is the _____?
– It's in the cupboard.

Where are the _____?
– They are on the shelf.

→ books • game • pens • phone • rucksack • ruler • tablets • lamp

▶ Quiz

▶ AH S. 12–13

4 Listen and sing along. ▶ Audio 17–18

1 Dad, where is my homework?
2 It's in your book.
3 But where is my book?
4 On the shelf there – look!
5 It's not on the shelf.
6 Maybe it's under the chair.
7 But where is the chair?
8 Next to the table – there!
9 Here is the book.
10 But now I know …
11 Where is your homework?
12 It's in the dog – oh no!

thirteen 13

A new student

1 Cartoon: Listen and read along. ▶  Audio 19

2 Learning English

Etwas auf Deutsch erklären
- Übersetze nicht Wort für Wort.
- Erkläre nur das Wichtigste.
- Benutze deine eigenen Worte.
- Sieh dir das Schild rechts an und sage auf Deutsch:
  Wann ist das Geschäft geöffnet?
  Was ist das Angebot am Montag?

▶ AH S. 14

3 Look and find …

- the blue blazers
- the grey rucksack
- the windows
- the dolphins
- …

①

②

③

4 Watch the video. It's about the logo of Varndean School. ▶ Video 1

1 Dolphins are ▭.
   Dolphins can ▭.

   → clever • speak • work together

2 Do you like dolphins?
   Do you like the logo of Varndean School?

5 Life in Britain

> Das **Logo** der *Varndean School* besteht aus fünf farbigen Delfinen.
> Der Delfin gilt als kluges, freundliches und hilfsbereites Tier.
> Der Delfin soll ein Vorbild für die Schüler und Schülerinnen sein.
> Die *Varndean School* ist in Brighton. Brighton liegt am Meer und der Delfin lebt im Meer. Deshalb passt das Delfin-Logo gut zu Brighton und zu der *Varndean School*.
>
> - Hat eure Schule auch ein Logo?
> - Wo kann man das Logo sehen?
> - Wie sieht das Logo aus?
> - Was bedeutet das Logo?

▶ AH S. 15

fifteen **15**

New words and phrases

👁 💬 **Look and say.**  Hilfe

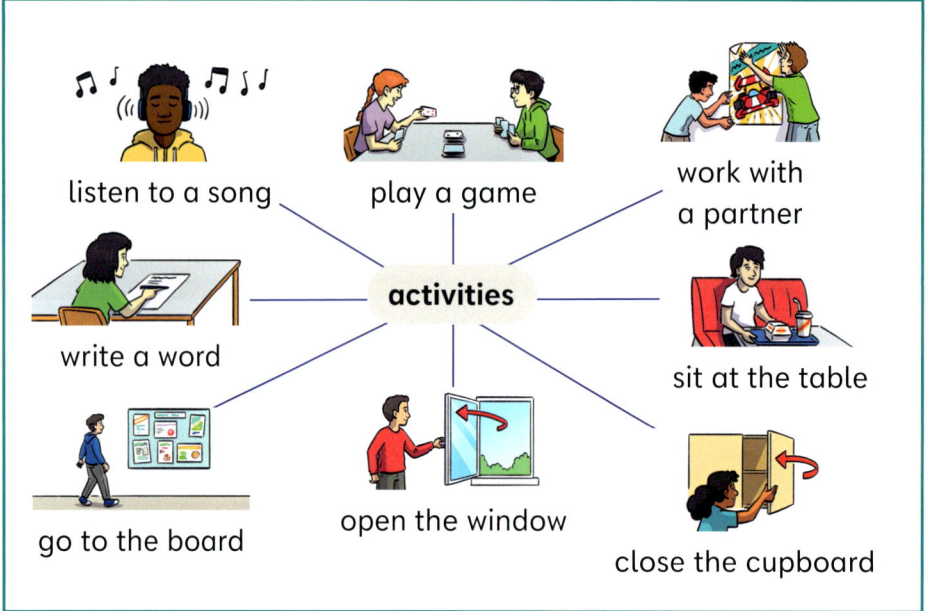

- listen to a song
- play a game
- work with a partner
- write a word
- **activities**
- sit at the table
- go to the board
- open the window
- close the cupboard

in · next to · on · under

She is a girl in my class.

He is a new boy in my class. He is from Germany.

So fragst du, ob du etwas tun darfst:

Can I work with Sunita?
Can I go to the board?
Can I open the window?
Can I write the word?

So fragst und sagst du, wo etwas ist:

Where is my phone?
– **It's** on the table.

Where are the books?
– **They are** in the cupboard.

▶ AH S. 16

Task: Learn words with a mind map

👁 **Step 1** Look at the mind map.

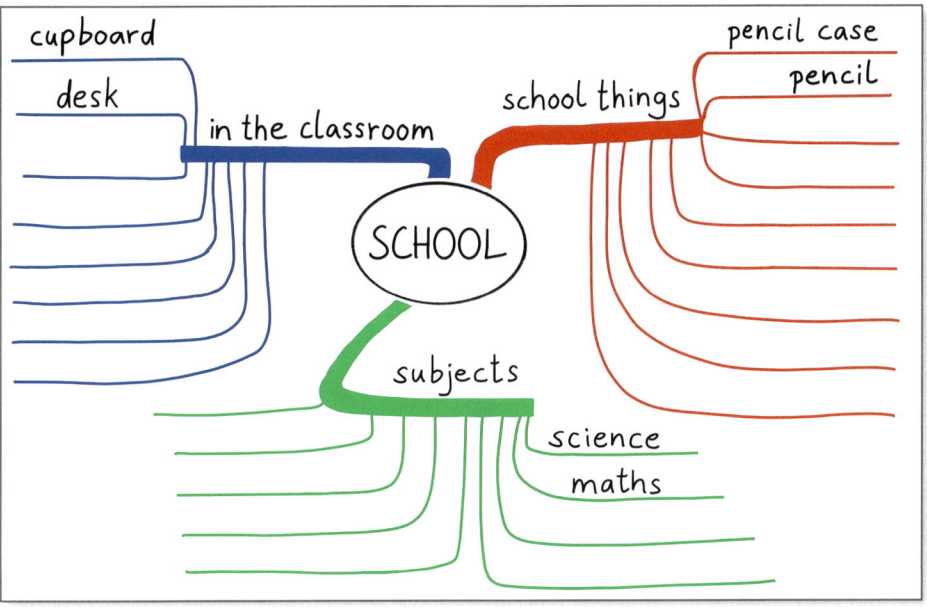

👥✏ **Step 2** Prepare your mind map. Work with a partner.   ▶  Hilfe

Schreibe das **Thema** in die Mitte. Schreibe die **Oberbegriffe** auf die Seitenarme.

👥💬 **Step 3** Learn your words with your partner.

Mache ein Foto von der Mindmap. So kannst du auch allein damit üben.

seventeen **17**

Family and pets

1 Look and say.

I can see a table.

There is Sunita.
There are some apples.

→
- a table
- Sunita's brother Nish
- some sausages
- two dogs
- ?

2 Look and listen. ▶ Audio 20

- Where is Jay?
- How old is Priya?
- And you? How old are you?

3 Listen and repeat. ▶ Audio 21

grandmother · grandfather · aunt · uncle · cousin

guinea pig · 1 mouse – 2 mice · 1 fish – 2 fish · rabbit · pets

▶ Quiz

4 Play a game: Pick a pair.

▶ AH Bildkarten

"Mouse ... and fish." "Rabbit ... and rabbit!"

▶ AH S. 17

5 Learning English

Aufgaben gemeinsam machen: Think Pair Share
- **Think** Überlege allein. Mache Notizen.
- **Pair** Überlegt zu zweit. Macht gemeinsam Notizen.
- **Share** Vergleicht eure Ergebnisse in der Gruppe oder Klasse.

Probiert es aus: Schreibt englische Wörter für Haustiere *(pets)* auf.

▶ Hilfe

nineteen 19

Family and pets

1 a) Listen to Lily and Sunita. ▶ Audio 22

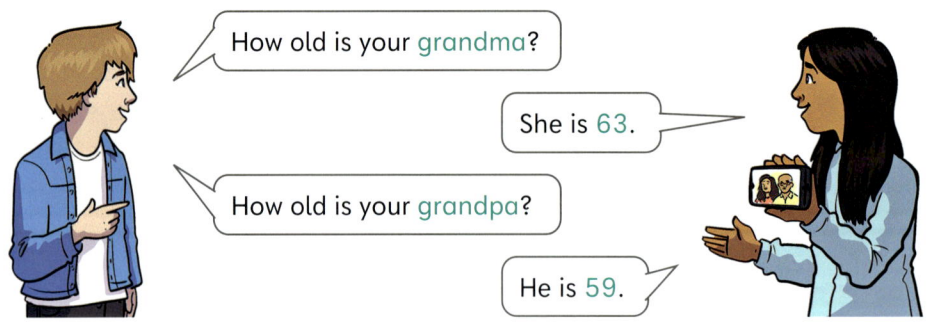

b) Now you: Ask and answer.

How old is your ⬚⬚⬚?
– He / She is 55.

> grandmother → grandma
> grandfather → grandpa
> mother → mum
> father → dad

▶ Numbers S. 85

▶ Quiz
▶ AH S. 18

2 a) Listen to Sunita and Noah. ▶ Audio 23

b) Now you: Ask and answer.

What's your ⬚⬚⬚'s name? → aunt • uncle • cousin • sister • brother • grandmother • ?
– Her name is Alina.

What's your ⬚⬚⬚'s name?
– His name is Ben.

▶ Hilfe
▶ Quiz
▶ AH S. 19

🎧 💬 **3 Listen and repeat.** ▶  Audio 24

cooking　　dancing　　gardening　　playing cards　　organizing

🎧 **4 a) Listen to Noah, Zane and Sunita.** ▶  Audio 25

I'm good at gardening. What about you?

I'm good at organizing. What about Lily?

She is good at running.

👥💬 **b) Now you: Ask and answer.**

I'm good at _____.
What about you?
– I'm good at _____.

What about Alina / Ben?
– She is good at _____.
– He is good at _____.

→ cooking • gardening • dancing • playing cards • organizing • cycling • playing football • ?

▶  Hilfe

▶  Quiz
▶ AH S. 20–21

🎧 **5 Listen and sing along.** ▶ Audio 26–27

1. I have a lot of pets in my house:
2. A fish, cat, dog, rabbit and mouse.
3. My fish is good at swimming.
4. My cat is good at chilling.
5. My dog is good at running.
6. My rabbit is good at jumping.
7. And my mouse is good at playing
8. Computer games!

twenty-one　21

Family and pets

1 a) Cartoon: Listen and read along.  Audio 28

b) Look and answer.
- Where is Bert?
- Where are Mert and Luke?

2 Now you: Make notes and talk.

Think. → Pair. → Share.

What are your 4 favourite pet names?

– I / We like ▭▭▭. What about you?
– We like ▭▭▭, ▭▭▭, ▭▭▭ and ▭▭▭.

▶ AH S. 22

  3 Look and find …

- King Charles III.
- Queen Camilla
- the red uniforms

 4 Listen and answer.  Audio 29

1. What are the King's favourite pets?
2. What are his favourite hobbies?
3. What is he good at?

- Ich höre den Text einmal.
- Ich lese die Fragen. Was soll ich herausfinden?
- Ich höre den Text genau.
- Ich beantworte die Fragen. Was weiß ich jetzt?

▶ Hör-Profi 2–3
S. 72

 5 Life in Britain

Charles III. („Charles der Dritte") ist König von Großbritannien und Nordirland. Am 6. Mai 2023 wurde die Krönung von Charles III. mit einem großen Fest gefeiert.
König Charles III. setzt sich für den Umweltschutz ein. Er möchte ein Vorbild sein: Er spart Energie und isst wenig Fleisch. Früher sammelte er Müll, zusammen mit seinen Söhnen William und Harry.
- Was machst du gerne draußen in der Natur?
- Was macht ihr in eurer Schule für den Umweltschutz?

▶ AH S. 23

twenty-three 23

New words and phrases

👁 💬 **Look and say.**  Hilfe

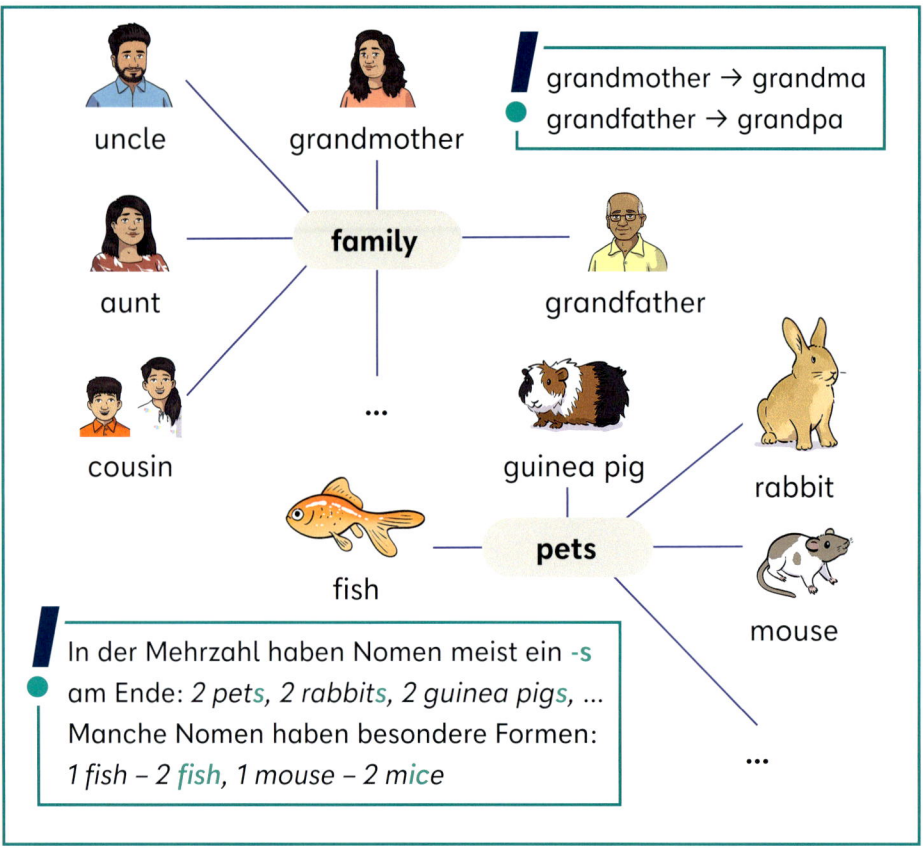

! grandmother → grandma
grandfather → grandpa

! In der Mehrzahl haben Nomen meist ein **-s** am Ende: 2 pet**s**, 2 rabbit**s**, 2 guinea pig**s**, … Manche Nomen haben besondere Formen:
1 fish – 2 *fish*, 1 mouse – 2 m*ice*

organizing dancing cooking gardening playing cards

So fragst und sagst du, wie alt jemand ist:	*So fragst und sagst du, wie jemand heißt:*	*So sagst du, dass du etwas gut kannst oder jemand etwas gut kann:*
How old is your cousin? – He is 17. – She is 12.	What's your cousin's name? – **His** name is Ben. – **Her** name is Lia.	**I'm** good at organizing. **He is** good at cooking. **She is** good at dancing.

▶ AH S. 24

Task: My favourite person

Step 1 Look and listen.  Audio 30

My favourite person is my brother.
His name is Samir.
He is 16.
He is good at cooking
and organizing.
Samir is great.

Step 2 Make notes about your favourite person.

Mache **Notizen**.
Die Notizen helfen dir,
frei zu sprechen.

- cousin
- Tina
- 17
- good at gaming
- clever

Step 3 Listen. Practise with a partner.  Audio 31

My favourite person
is my cousin.
Her name is Tina.
She is 17.
She is good at gaming.
Tina is clever.

Step 4 Tell your class about your favourite person.

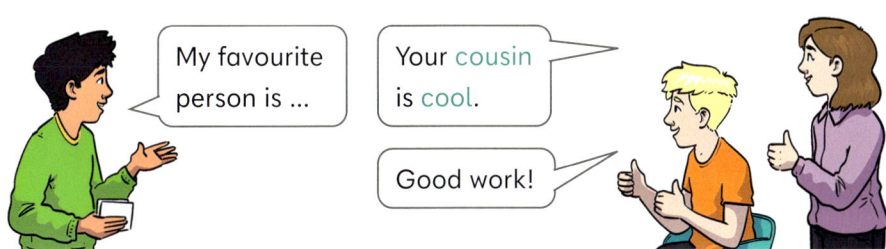

My favourite person is …

Your cousin is cool.

Good work!

▶ Classroom English S. 84

Body

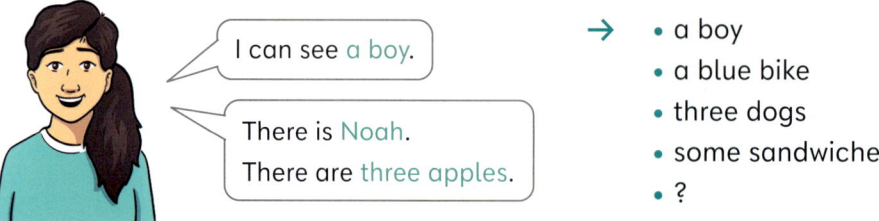

👁💬 **1** Look and say.

I can see a boy.

There is Noah.
There are three apples.

→
- a boy
- a blue bike
- three dogs
- some sandwiches
- ?

👁👂 **2** Look and listen. ▶ Audio 32

1 Who are Luna, Rocky and Nono?
– Luna, Rocky and Nono are ▭ ▭.
2 Who is Leo? – Leo is Noah's ▭.
3 What's a great idea? – ▭ is a great idea.

3 Listen and repeat. ▶ Audio 33

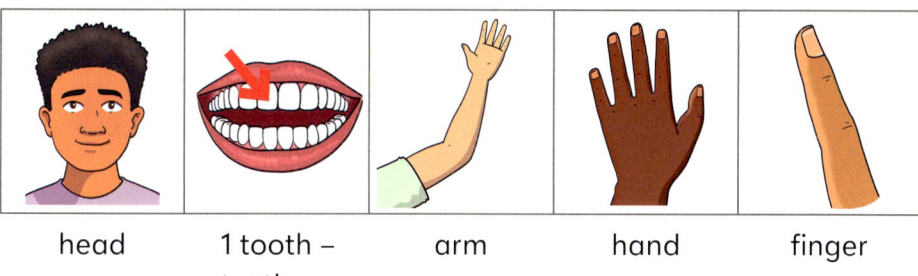

| head | 1 tooth – teeth | arm | hand | finger |

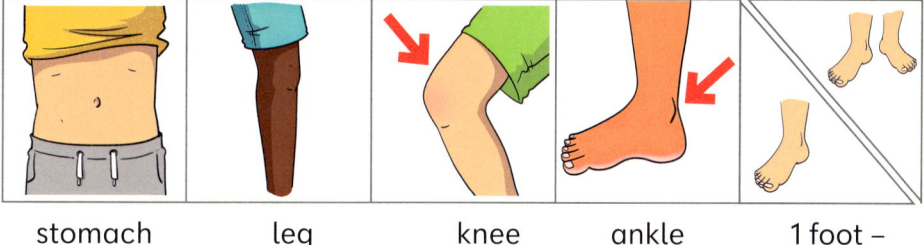

| stomach | leg | knee | ankle | 1 foot – 2 feet |

▶ Quiz

- Ich höre das Wort mehrmals. Wie klingt das Wort?
- Ich spreche leise mit.
- Ich spreche das Wort laut nach. Wie klingt es bei mir?

▶ Sprech-Profi 1–2 S. 73

▶ AH S. 25–26

4 Play a game: Simon says …

▶ AH Bildkarten

Simon says: Touch your head.

Simon says: Touch your legs.

twenty-seven 27

Body

1 a) Listen to Lily, Noah and Zane.  Audio 34

Are you OK?

Yes, I am.

No, I'm not. My arm hurts.

b) Now you: Ask and answer.

Are you OK?

- Yes, I am.
- No, I'm not.
 My ▭ hurts.

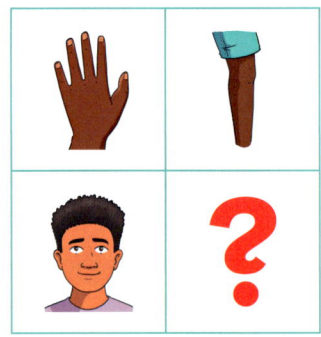

 Quiz
▶ AH S. 27

2 Learning English

▶ AH Bildkarten

Englisch lernen mit den Bildkarten
- Lerne immer 5–10 Wörter auf einmal.
- Lege die Karten vor dich hin.
- Nimm eine Karte und decke das Wort ab.
- Sieh das Bild an und sage das Wort laut.
- Du kannst das Wort? Lege die Karte zur Seite.
- Du bist unsicher? Sieh das Wort genau an und sage es laut.
- Du kannst das Wort in der **App** noch mal hören.
- Probiere es mit den Wörtern von S. 27 aus.

▶ AH S. 28 Nr. 1

3 Listen and repeat.

Quiz

4 a) Listen to Zane and his mother.

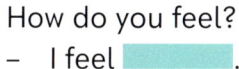 **b)** Now you: Ask and answer.

How do you feel? → hot • cold • tired • sick • good • not so good • ?
– I feel ▬▬▬.

▶ Hilfe

▶ Quiz

▶ AH S. 28 Nr. 2–3; S. 29

5 Listen and sing along.

1 Move your body,
2 One, two, three,
3 Move your body
4 Just like me.

5 Touch your head,
6 Touch your feet,
7 Smile and show me
8 All your teeth!

9 Move your fingers,
10 Clap your hands,
11 Turn around,
12 Yes, you can!

13 Touch your stomach,
14 Touch your knee,
15 Move your body
16 Just like me.

twenty-nine **29**

Body

1 Cartoon: Listen and read along. ▶ Audio 39

- What's "ambulance" in German?
- What's the phone number of the ambulance in Britain?

2 Look and listen. Say it in German. ▶ Audio 40

Etwas auf Deutsch erklären
- Übersetze nicht Wort für Wort.
- Erkläre nur das Wichtigste.
- Benutze deine eigenen Worte.

▶ AH S. 30

3 Look, read and say.

The trail running club is on Thursday.
The teacher is Mr Green.
The club is for years 7 to 9.

 Hilfe

TRAIL RUNNING CLUB EVERY THURSDAY years 7–9 park Mr Green	BADMINTON CLUB EVERY TUESDAY years 8–10 sports hall Ms May
GIRLS RUGBY CLUB EVERY MONDAY years 7–11 rugby pitch Ms Singh	CRICKET CLUB EVERY WEDNESDAY years 7–11 sports field Mr Summer

4 Watch the video. It's about sports at Varndean School.  Video 2

- What sports can you see in the video?
- Where is the sports field?

5 Life in Britain

An der *Varndean School* und an den meisten Schulen in Großbritannien ist **Sport** sehr wichtig. Im Sportunterricht lernen die Schüler und Schülerinnen viele Sportarten kennen. Die *school clubs* bieten weitere Sportarten an, zum Beispiel Cricket und Rugby.
- Welche Sportangebote in deiner Schule magst du?
- Würdest du gerne Cricket oder Rugby ausprobieren?

▶ AH S. 31

New words and phrases

Look and say.  Hilfe

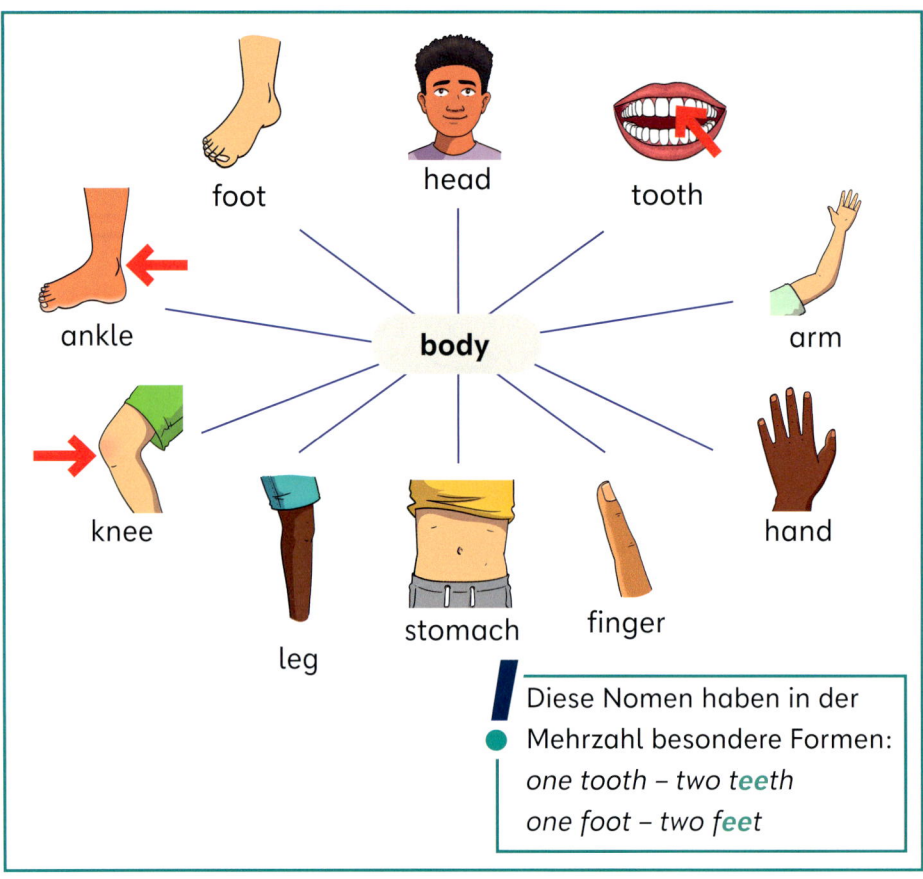

Diese Nomen haben in der Mehrzahl besondere Formen:
*one tooth – two t**ee**th*
*one foot – two f**ee**t*

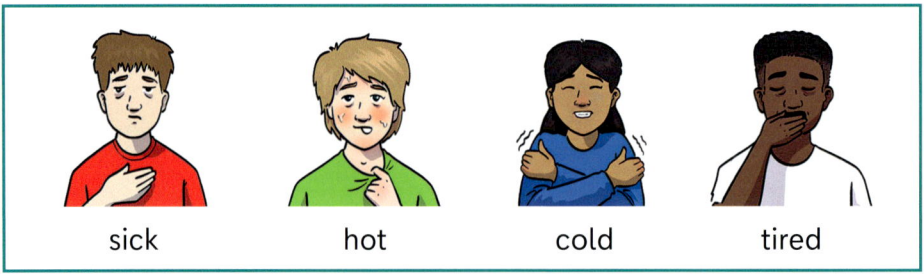

So fragst du, ob alles in Ordnung ist:

Are you OK?
– Yes, I am.
– No, I'm not.

So sagst du, was dir wehtut:

My arm hurts.
My tooth hurts.

So fragst du, wie sich jemand fühlt:

How do you feel?
– I feel tired.

▶ AH S. 32

Task: A dialogue with the doctor

Step 1 Watch the video.

 Video 3

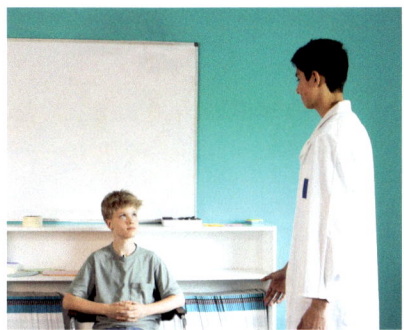

Einen Dialog vorspielen
- Spielt möglichst auswendig.
- Seht euch beim Sprechen an.
- Sprecht laut und deutlich.
- Seht euch das Video an: Beachten die Jungen diese drei Regeln?

Step 2 Pick your roles. Prepare and practise your dialogue.

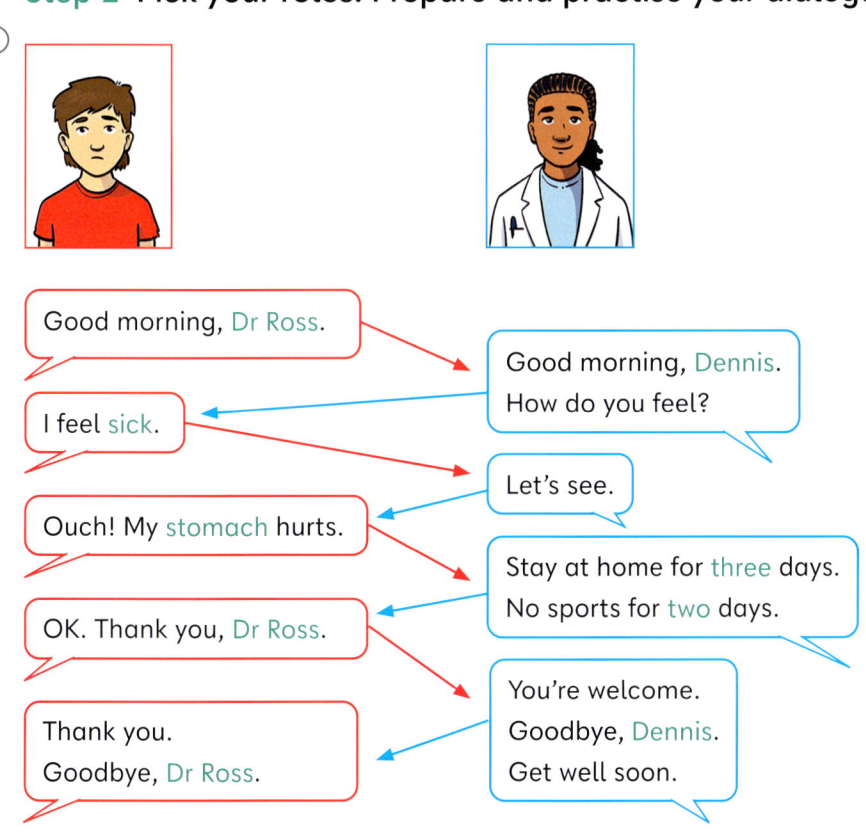

Good morning, Dr Ross.

Good morning, Dennis. How do you feel?

I feel sick.

Let's see.

Ouch! My stomach hurts.

Stay at home for three days. No sports for two days.

OK. Thank you, Dr Ross.

You're welcome. Goodbye, Dennis. Get well soon.

Thank you. Goodbye, Dr Ross.

Step 3 Act out your dialogue.

- **Spielende:** Achtet auf die drei Regeln von **Step 1**.
- **Zuschauende:** Gebt Feedback. Wurden die drei Regeln beachtet?

Friends

1 Look and say.

I can see a skatepark.

There is a sandwich.
There are two blue chairs.

→
- a skatepark
- a pink T-shirt
- skateboards
- white sneakers
- ?

2 Look and listen.  Audio 41

- What would Zane like?
- Where is the new takeaway?
- What is Bill good at?

3 Listen and repeat. ▶ Audio 42

| friend | hair | blond | long | short |

| eye | glasses | braces | helpful | honest |

▶ Quiz

4 Play a game: Picture bingo

▶ AH Bildkarten

Glasses.

Bingo!

5 Listen. Talk to a partner. ▶ Audio 43

I have short blond hair.
I have blue eyes.

I have long black hair.
I have brown eyes.

▶ AH S. 33–34

thirty-five 35

Friends

1 a) Listen to Zane and his grandpa.

Tell me about your friends Lily and Finn.

Finn has short brown hair and brown eyes. He is nice.

Lily has short blond hair and green eyes. She is honest.

b) Now you: Tell your partner about Rick, Amy and Jack.

Tell me about Rick.
- He has ▬▬▬▬.
- He is ▬▬▬▬.

Tell me about Amy.
- She has ▬▬▬▬.
- She is ▬▬▬▬.

Rick   Amy   Jack

▶ Hilfe

▶ Quiz
▶ AH S. 35

2 Listen and rap along. ▶ Audio 45–46

1 Meet my best friend:
2 Her name's Dee.
3 She has long hair
4 To her knee!
5 She is helpful
6 And she's cool.
7 We play football
8 After school.

9 Meet my best friend:
10 He's so nice.
11 He has blond hair
12 And green eyes.
13 His name's Malik.
14 He has braces.
15 He likes making
16 Funny faces!

Tipp
name's = name is
she's = she is
he's = he is

36 thirty-six

3 a) Listen to Aunt Priya, Sunita and Nish. ▶ Audio 47

Speech bubbles: "What do you do with your friends?" – "We watch videos." – "We play football."

b) Now you: Ask and answer.

What do you do with your friends? →

– We watch videos.

We
- watch videos.
- watch films.
- play football.
- play computer games.
- go to the cinema.
- go to the youth centre.
- listen to music.
- chill.
- ?

▶ Hilfe
▶ Quiz
▶ AH S. 36

4 Learning English

> **Ähnliche Wörter im Englischen und in anderen Sprachen**
> - Manche Wörter sind im Englischen ähnlich wie in anderen Sprachen.
> - Diese Wörter kannst du dir besonders gut merken.
> - Die englischen Wörter werden oft anders ausgesprochen oder geschrieben.
> - Vergleiche *long, blond, friend, hair* mit den deutschen Wörtern.
> - Vergleiche *football, cinema* mit den türkischen Wörtern.
> - Fallen dir noch andere Beispiele ein?
>
> **TIPP**: Verwende eine **Wörterbuch-App**.
> Dort kannst du die Wörter auch anhören.

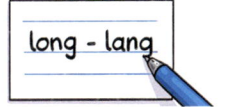

▶ Quiz
▶ AH S. 37

thirty-seven **37**

Friends

  1 a) Cartoon: Listen and read along.

 b) Read and answer.

- Where are Zane and Finn?
- Who is Marek?

- Ich höre den Text und lese mit. Was verstehe ich?
- Ich lese die Fragen. Was soll ich herausfinden?
- Ich lese den Text genau. Ich achte auf die Schlüsselwörter.
- Ich beantworte die Fragen.

▶ Lese-Profi 2–3
S. 74

▶ AH S. 38

2 Look and say.

1 What activities can friends do in Brighton?
   – Friends can chill at the beach.

2 What activities can you and your friends do in your town?
   – We can ▓▓▓▓▓▓ too. We can ▓▓▓▓▓▓.

chill at the beach

go to Brighton Pier

play darts at the youth centre

go to the shops

3 Watch the video. It's about a youth centre in Brighton. ▶ Video 4

- What's Sunita good at?
- What's Lily good at?

4 Life in Britain

> Teenager in Großbritannien treffen sich mit ihren Freunden zu Hause oder draußen, zum Beispiel im Park oder beim Sport.
> In Brighton gibt es **Jugendzentren** (*youth centres*), in denen sich Kinder und Jugendliche treffen können. Dort gibt es viele Angebote: Theater, Filmschnitt, Graffiti, Tanzen, Klettern und vieles mehr.
> - Wo triffst du dich mit deinen Freunden?
> - Welche Angebote gibt es in deiner Nähe?

▶ AH S. 39

New words and phrases

Look and say.  Hilfe

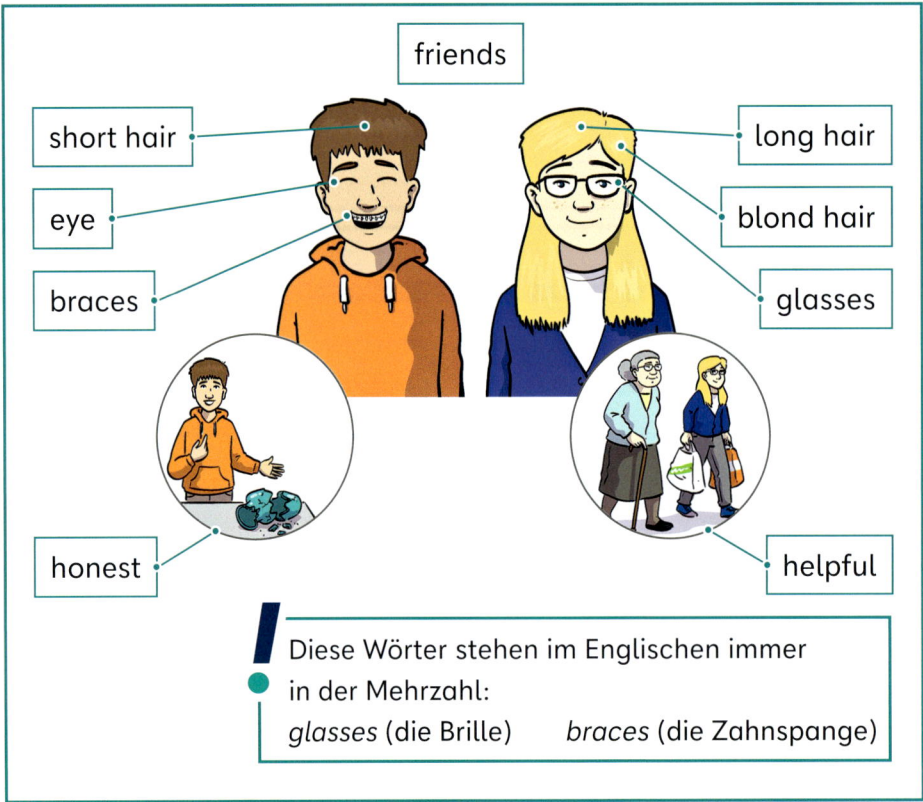

! Diese Wörter stehen im Englischen immer in der Mehrzahl:
glasses (die Brille)   *braces* (die Zahnspange)

So bittest du jemanden, von etwas zu erzählen:

Tell me about your friend.
Tell me about your hobbies.

So beschreibst du jemanden:

He has short blond hair.
He is helpful.
She has brown eyes.
She is honest.

So fragst du, was jemand mit seinen Freunden macht. Und so antwortest du:

What do you do with your friends?
– **We watch** films and videos.
– **We play** computer games.
– **We go** to the cinema and **we chill**.

▶ AH S. 40

Task: Who is it?

Step 1 Watch the video.

 Video 5

My friend has short brown hair.
My friend has green eyes.
My friend is helpful.
He is funny.
He is good at running.
We play football and we chill.

Step 2 Prepare your slide show.

1. Write 5 sentences or more.
2. Animate your sentences.

My friend has long black hair.
My friend has brown eyes.
My friend is

1. My friend has long black hair.
2. My friend has brown eyes.
3. My friend is clever.
4. She is funny.
5. She is good at drawing.

- Ich sehe mir die Sätze in **Step 1** genau an.
- Ich schreibe die Sätze sorgfältig ab.
- Ich ersetze die blauen Wörter durch meine eigenen Ideen.

▶ Schreib-Profi 1–2 S. 75

Step 3 Practise your presentation.

Benutze beim Üben eine **Aufnahme-App**:
Nimm deine Sätze auf und höre sie an. Hast du deutlich gesprochen?

Step 4 Present your slide show to the class.

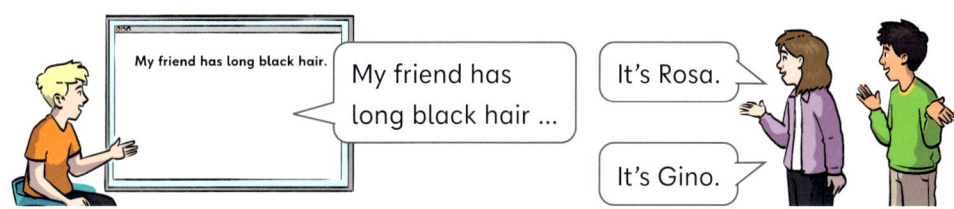

forty-one 41

Food and drinks

👁💬 **1** Look and say.

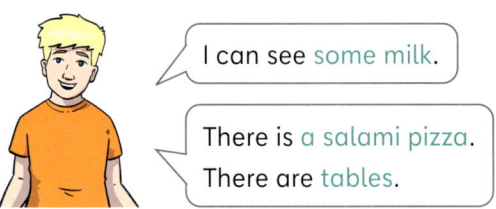

I can see some milk.

There is a salami pizza.
There are tables.

→
- some juice
- a green apple
- a veggie pizza
- some red apples
- ?

👁👂 **2** Look and listen.

- What day is it?
- Who would like an egg sandwich?
- Who would like a veggie pizza?

3 Listen and repeat.

▶ Audio 50

| chicken | ham | pasta | chips | yoghurt |

| salad | tomato | banana | lemonade | ice tea |

▶ Quiz
▶ AH S. 41–42

4 Play a game: What's missing?

▶ AH Bildkarten

What's missing? — The ice tea.

! Beginnt ein Wort mit den Vokalen **a**, **e**, **i**, **o** , **u**, dann wird **the** meist anders ausgesprochen. Höre es dir in der **App** an.

▶ Hilfe

5 Listen. Ask and answer.

▶ Audio 51

Do you like yoghurt? — Yes, I do.
Do you like tomatoes? — No, I don't.

forty-three 43

Food and drinks

1 a) Listen to Noah, Lily and Zane.  Audio 52

b) Now you: Ask and answer.

Do you eat ▭?
– Yes, I do.
– No, I don't.
 But I eat ▭.

Do you drink ▭?
– Yes, I do.
– No, I don't.
 But I drink ▭.

▶ Hilfe
▶ Quiz
▶ AH S. 43

2 Listen and sing along.  Audio 53–54

1 Time for dinner.
2 What would you like? (2x)

3 Would you like pizza
4 With tomatoes and cheese?
5 I don't eat that.
6 No pizza, please!

7 Do you eat chicken?
8 It's nice to eat.
9 No, I don't.
10 I don't eat meat!

11 Do you drink lemonade
12 Or maybe ice tea?
13 No, I don't.
14 Just water for me!

15 Would you like sandwiches
16 With butter and honey?
17 Oh yes, please.
18 They are yummy!

44 forty-four

3 Listen and repeat. ▶ Audio 55

| mushroom | pepper | onion | tuna | corn |

▶ Quiz
▶ AH S. 44

4 a) Listen to Noah and his father. ▶ Audio 56

What does Lily eat?
Lily eats tomatoes. She doesn't eat mushrooms.
What does Zane drink?
Zane drinks lemonade. He doesn't drink ice tea.

b) Now you: Look at the list. Ask and answer.

What does Lily eat / drink?
– Lily ea**t**s tomatoes.
– She **doesn't** eat _____.
– She drink**s** _____.
– She **doesn't** drink _____.

What does Zane eat / drink?
– Zane eat**s** tomatoes.
– He **doesn't** eat _____.
– He drink**s** _____.
– He **doesn't** drink _____.

	Lily	Zane
tomatoes	✓	✓
mushrooms	✗	✓
onions	✓	✗
tuna	✗	✓
peppers	✗	✓
ice tea	✓	✗
lemonade	✗	✓

▶ Quiz
▶ AH S. 45

forty-five

Food and drinks

1 Cartoon: Listen and read along.  Audio 57

- What's mattar paneer?
- What does Lily eat?

Panel 1: Dinner is on the table. Lily, would you like some mattar paneer?

Panel 2: Yes, thank you. What is it?

Panel 3: It's Indian food.

Panel 4: Do you eat tomatoes?

Panel 5: Yes, I do. But I don't eat peppers.

Panel 6: That looks good. Is it chicken?

Panel 7: No, it's cheese.

Panel 8: We don't eat chicken.

Panel 9: Lily, would you like some more?

Panel 10: Hey, this is my favourite food!

2 Look and read. Use the internet.

1. Is mattar paneer in photo ① or photo ②?
2. What's "paneer" in English?

 ①
 ②

▶ AH S. 46

3 Learning English

> **Englische Texte verstehen**
> - Wenn du englische Texte liest, musst du nicht jedes Wort kennen.
> - Sieh dir die Bilder an.
> - Denke an ähnliche Wörter in anderen Sprachen.
> - Benutze eine **Wörterbuch-App**.
> - Probiere es mit der Speisekarte in Aufgabe 4 aus.

4 Look and read.

Burgers	Pizza
• beef • chicken • veggie	• small • medium • large
Fish and chips	mild medium hot
• small • medium • large with vinegar or with ketchup	• salami • mushroom • pepper • spinach

5 Watch the video. It's about Zane's family and food.

 Video 6

What is on Zane's *favourite pizza*?

6 Life in Britain

> In Großbritannien sind ***fish and chips*** sehr beliebt. Viele Menschen essen auch gern Burger, Pizza, Tacos, Currys oder Kebab.
> - Was isst du gern? Woher kommt dieses Essen?

▶ AH S. 47

New words and phrases

Look and say.  Hilfe

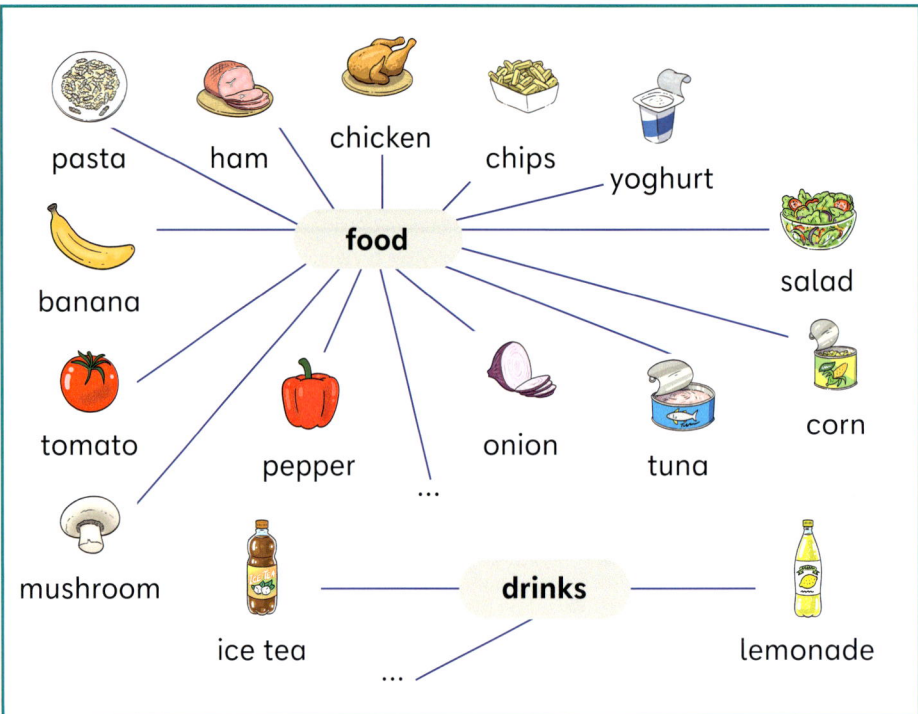

So sagst du, was du isst und trinkst:

Do you eat mushrooms?
– Yes, I do.
– No, I don't.
  But I eat onions.

Do you drink ice tea?
– Yes, I do.
– No, I don't.
  But I drink lemonade.

So sagst du, was jemand (nicht) isst oder (nicht) trinkt:

What does Noah eat?
– He eat**s** ham.
– He **doesn't** eat chicken.

What does Sunita drink?
– She drink**s** ice tea.
– She **doesn't** drink lemonade.

> ❗ Wenn du über jemand anderes sprichst, hängst du ein **-s** an das Verb an: drink**s**, eat**s**, like**s**.
> Merke dir:
> *He, she, it* – das **-s** muss mit!

▶ AH S. 48

Task: An invitation to a pizza party

👁 📖 **Step 1** Look and read.

PIZZA PARTY Invitation for Luca	Please tick.	
	Do you eat …?	Do you drink …?
where: at the youth centre day: Friday time: 5 o'clock Can you come?	☑ peppers ☑ onions ☑ ham ☑ mushrooms	☑ water ☑ apple juice ☑ lemonade ☑ ice tea

✋ ✏ **Step 2** Pick words for food and drinks. Write your invitation.

food	drinks
peppers salami corn	lemonade ice tea water

- Ich sehe mir die Einladung in **Step 1** genau an.
- Ich schreibe eine ähnliche Einladung.
- Ich ersetze die blauen Wörter durch meine eigenen Ideen.

▶ Schreib-Profi 1–2 S. 75

👥 💬 **Step 3** Give your infitation to a partner.   ▶ 👆 Hilfe

Here is my invitation for you, Luca.

Thank you, Ella.

Here is my invitation for you, Rico.

Thank you, Amira.

forty-nine 49

My week

1 Look and say.

I can see a phone.

There is a rucksack.
There are students.

→
- a phone
- a park
- windows
- students
- ?

2 Look and listen.  Audio 58

- Is Lily OK?
- Where is Finn's science homework?
- What is the science teacher's name?
- And you? Do you like Mondays?

3 Listen and repeat. ▶ Audio 59

meet friends | walk the dog | go shopping | go swimming | do sport

do my homework | make dinner | help my dad | look after my sister | clean my room

▶ Quiz

4 Play a game: Pick a pair.

▶ AH Bildkarten

Meet friends ... and make dinner.

Do sport ... and do sport!

▶ AH S. 49

5 Listen. Talk to a partner. ▶ Audio 60

I meet friends every Monday.

I look after my brother every Thursday.

▶ AH S. 50

fifty-one 51

My week

1 a) Listen to Zane and Lily. ▶ Audio 61

b) Now you: Listen. Ask and answer. ▶ Audio 62

What about Monday?
– Noah helps his dad every Monday.

→

Noah	help**s** his dad walk**s** the dog	every Monday. every Tuesday.
Sunita	clean**s** her room d**oes** her homework g**oes** shopping	every Wednesday. every Thursday. every Friday.

▶ Quiz
▶ AH S. 51;
S. 52 Nr. 1

2 Listen and sing along. ▶ Audio 63–64

1. Every Monday, Mo goes swimming.
2. Every Tuesday, he helps his mother.
3. Every Wednesday, he cleans his room.
4. Every Thursday, he looks after his brother.
5. Every Friday, he does his homework.
6. Every Saturday, he meets his friends.
7. Every Sunday, he watches a film.
8. And then it starts again …

> Achte auf die Aussprache von -s und -es am Ende der Verben.

3 a) Listen to Lily and her friends. ▶ Audio 65

b) Now you: Ask and answer.

What's the time?

– It's 7 o'clock.
– It's 9.30.

▶ Hilfe

▶ Quiz

▶ AH S. 52 Nr. 2; S. 53 Nr. 3

4 Listen. Now you: Talk in class. ▶ Audio 66

▶ Quiz

▶ AH S. 53 Nr. 4

fifty-three 53

My week

  1 a) Cartoon: Listen and read along.

  b) Read and answer.

- When do Lily and Zane meet?
- When is Zane's video club?

Let's go cycling on Saturday.

I go to the video club every Saturday.

Can we meet at 2 o'clock?

Good idea.

What about Finn?

He looks after his brother every Saturday.

Oh no! My bike is dirty.

I can help you.

Thanks, Lily! What's the time, please?

It's 3.30.

Oh no! My video club starts at 4 o'clock. Sorry, Lily!

- Ich lese die Fragen. Was soll ich herausfinden?
- Ich lese den Text genau. Ich achte auf die Schlüsselwörter.
- Ich beantworte die Fragen.
- Ich überlege zum Schluss:
  - Was ist in der Geschichte passiert?
  - Was hat mir geholfen, die Geschichte zu verstehen?

▶ Lese-Profi 2–3 S. 74

▶ AH S. 54

2 Look. Say the days of the week.

MON	TUE	WED	THU	FRI	SAT	SUN

3 a) Read and find ...

- the days of the week
- the name of the band

b) Find the song on the internet. Listen to it.

Is the music **happy**?   Or is the music **sad**?

Friday I'm in love

1 I don't care if Monday's blue
2 Tuesday's grey and Wednesday too
3 Thursday I don't care about you
4 It's Friday, I'm in love

5 Monday you can fall apart
6 Tuesday, Wednesday, break my heart
7 Oh, Thursday doesn't even start
8 It's Friday, I'm in love (...)

(from a song by The Cure, words by Robert Smith)

4 Songs in English

Viele **Songs**, die wir hören, sind auf Englisch. Das liegt auch daran, dass Englisch eine Weltsprache ist: Menschen auf der ganzen Welt können sich auf Englisch verständigen.
- Welche Songs gefallen dir?
- Hörst du auch Songs auf Englisch?
- Suche im Internet englische Songs mit Wochentagen.

▶ AH S. 55

fifty-five

New words and phrases

👁 💬 **Look and say.**  Hilfe

	meet friends		do my homework
	walk the dog		help my dad
	do sport		make dinner
	go swimming		look after my sister
	go shopping		clean my room

So sagst du, was jemand jeden Montag, Dienstag, … tut:

Zane	meet**s** friends	every Monday.
Noah	walk**s** the dog	every Tuesday.
Lily	clean**s** her room	every Wednesday.
Finn	make**s** dinner	every Thursday.
Zane	do**es** sport	every Friday.
Lily	go**es** shopping	every Saturday.
Finn	go**es** swimming	every Sunday.

❙● In der Regel hängst du ein **-s** an das Verb an: *meet**s**, clean**s**, walk**s**.* Manchmal setzt du ein **-e-** davor: *do**es**, go**es**.*

So fragst du nach der Uhrzeit und sagst du die Uhrzeit:

What's the time, please?
– It's 7 o'clock.
– It's 7.15.
– It's 7.30.
– It's 7.45.

❙● *7 o'clock* kann „7 Uhr morgens" und „7 Uhr abends" bedeuten.

So verabredest du dich für einen Tag und eine Uhrzeit:

Let's meet on Friday at 5 o'clock.
– Good idea.
– Sorry, I can't. I help my mum every Friday.

▶ AH S. 56

Task: Make plans to meet friends

Step 1 Watch the video.   ▶  Video 7

Let's go to the cinema this week.
– Good idea!

What about Saturday at 11 o'clock?
– Sorry, I can't. I look after my sister every Saturday.

What about Sunday at 4 o'clock?
– OK. Great!

Step 2 Pick ideas. Practise with a partner. Copy the table.

- go to the cinema
- go cycling
- watch videos
- play football

	Saturday	Sunday
11.00		
4.00		

- Nimm einen Bleistift und ein Lineal. Zeichne die **Tabelle** ab.
- Trage mit einem roten Stift ein, wann du nicht kannst.
- In die 3 freien Felder trägst du deine Verabredungen ein (bei **Step 3**).

	Saturday	Sunday
11.00	do sport	Rico

Step 3 Walk around. Make plans with 2 different partners.

Let's play football this week.

Good idea!

What about Saturday at 4 o'clock?

Sorry, I can't. I have plans with Luca.

What about Sunday at 11 o'clock?

OK. Great!

Shopping

1 Look and say.

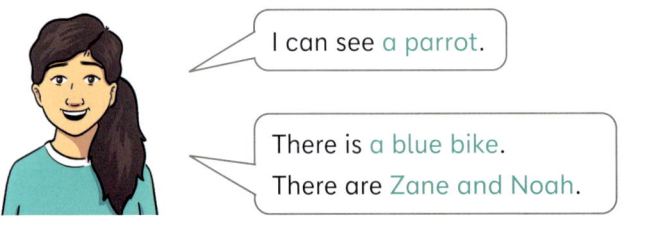

I can see a parrot.

There is a blue bike.
There are Zane and Noah.

→
- a parrot
- a girl
- shops
- books
- ?

2 Look and listen.  Audio 68

- What colour is the cushion for Sunita's birthday?
- When is Sunita's birthday party?
- Where is the party?

58 fifty-eight

3 Listen and repeat. ▶ Audio 69

cap · jeans · trousers · sweatshirt · shorts

skirt · socks · shoes · jacket · clothes

▶ Quiz
▶ AH S. 57

4 Play a game: Picture bingo

▶ AH Bildkarten

A skirt. — Bingo!

5 Listen. Ask and answer. ▶ Audio 70

Do you like the white cap? — Yes, I do. — Do you like the black jeans? — No, I don't. But I like the blue jeans.

▶ AH S. 58

fifty-nine 59

Shopping

1 a) Listen to Zane and the shop assistant.  Audio 71

b) Now you: Ask and answer.

Does the ▬▬▬ fit?
– Yes, it does. Thanks.
– No, it doesn't.
  It's too small.

Do the ▬▬▬ fit?
– Yes, they do. Thanks.
– No, they don't.
  They are too big.

▶ Hilfe

▶ Quiz
▶ AH S. 59–60

2 Listen and rap along.  Audio 72–73

1 Do you like the sweatshirt?
2 What about the green skirt?
3 No, the skirt's too long.
4 And the sweatshirt is wrong.
5 Does the jacket fit?
6 No, it's too big!
7 The trousers are too small.
8 They don't fit at all.

9 Do you like the shoes?
10 No, I don't – they're blue.
11 Well, what about the shorts?
12 Yes, they're great for sports!

Tipp
skirt's = skirt is
they're = they are

3 Listen and repeat.

   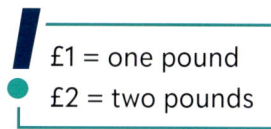

shop assistant — pay cash — pay by card — pounds

> £1 = one pound
> £2 = two pounds

▶  Audio 74

▶ Quiz

4 a) Listen to Zane and the shop assistant.

▶  Audio 75

How much is the cap? — It's 9 pounds.

How much are the socks? — They are 1 pound.

b) Now you: Ask and answer.

How much is the skirt?
– It's _____ pounds.

How much are the trousers?
– They are _____ pounds.

skirt	£16	trousers	£18
sweatshirt	£12	jeans	£14
jacket	£24	shoes	£25
cap	£9	sneakers	£29

▶ Hilfe

▶ Quiz
▶ AH S. 61

5 Learning English

Nach unbekannten Wörtern fragen
- Wenn du ein englisches Wort nicht weißt, kannst du jemanden höflich fragen:
  Excuse me, please. What's this in English?
- Probiere es aus: Zeige auf einen Gegenstand und frage nach dem englischen Wort.

▶ Hilfe

▶ Quiz

Shopping

1 a) Cartoon: Listen and read along.  Audio 76

- What is Nina's job?
- How much are the jeans?

b) Find a story ending. Act out the cartoon.

- Ich spreche die Sätze der letzten drei Bilder nach.
- Ich denke mir ein Ende für die Geschichte aus.
- Ich übe so lange, bis ich die Sätze sicher sagen kann.
- Ich achte auf meine Körpersprache.
- Welche Wörter oder Sätze will ich mir merken?

▶ Sprech-Profi 2–3 S. 73

▶ AH S. 62

2 Look and find ...

- 20 pounds
- 2 pounds
- 2 pence

3 Watch the video. It's about shopping. ▶ Video 8

- How much is the T-shirt?
- How much are the sneakers?

4 Life in Britain

In Großbritannien bezahlen die Menschen mit **pounds** (£) und **pence** (p). Das Pfund-Zeichen £ wird vor den Preis geschrieben. Ein Pfund sind 100 Pence.

Viele Menschen benutzen statt *pence* die Abkürzung *p* („pii"). Höre dir in der **App** an, wie das klingt.

▶  Hilfe

Seit 2024 sieht man auch König Charles III. auf Münzen und Geldscheinen.

- Hast du schon mit einer anderen Währung als Euro und Cent bezahlt?
- Welche Währungen kennst du noch?

▶ AH S. 63

New words and phrases

Look and say.  Hilfe

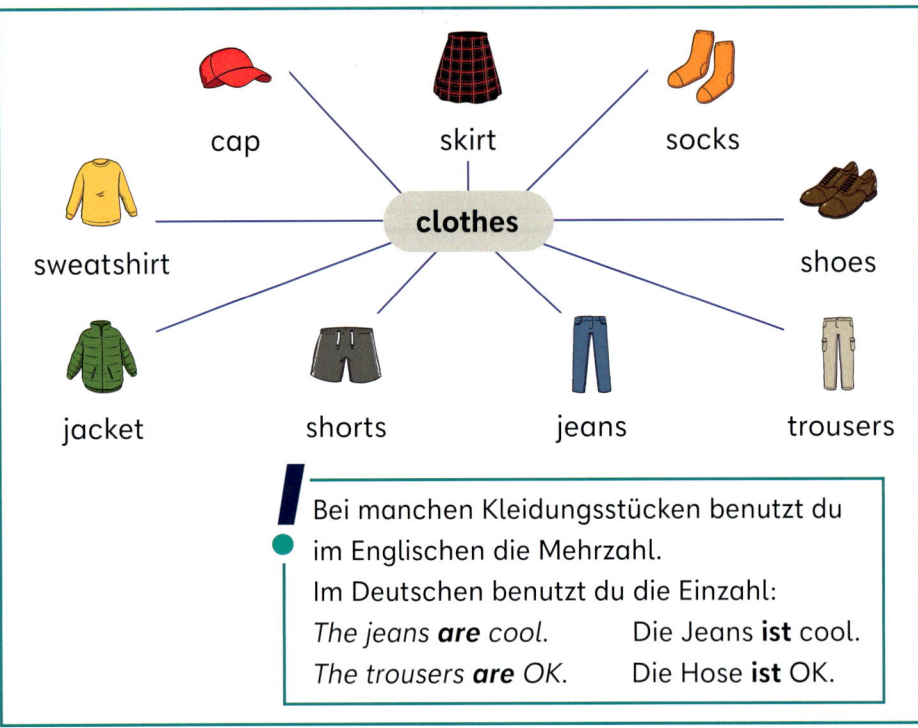

! Bei manchen Kleidungsstücken benutzt du im Englischen die Mehrzahl.
Im Deutschen benutzt du die Einzahl:
The jeans **are** *cool.*   Die Jeans **ist** cool.
The trousers **are** *OK.*   Die Hose **ist** OK.

So fragst und sagst du, ob etwas passt:

Does the jacket fit?
– Yes, **it does**. Thanks.
– No, **it doesn't**.
   It's too small.

Do the shoes fit?
– Yes, **they do**. Thanks.
– No, **they don't**.
   They are too big.

So fragst und sagst du, wieviel etwas kostet:

How much **is** the skirt?
– **It's** 18 pounds.

How much **are** the socks?
– **They are** one pound.

▶ AH S. 64

Task: A shopping dialogue

Step 1 Watch the video.

 Video 9

Hello. Can I help you?
– Hi. Yes, please.
　How much is the red T-shirt?
It's 8 pounds.
– OK. I like it.
Does the T-shirt fit?
– Yes, it does. Thanks.
Cash or card?
– Cash, please. Here you are. (…)

Step 2 Pick your roles. Prepare and practise your dialogue.

Hello! Can I help you?

Hi. Yes, please.
How much is the black T-shirt?

It's 9 pounds 50.

OK. I like it.

Does the T-shirt fit?

YES ↓　　　　**NO** ↓

Yes, it does. Thanks.

Cash or card?

By card, please. Here you are.

Thanks. Goodbye.

Bye.

What about the green T-shirt?

No, it doesn't. It's too big.

No, thanks. It's not so cool.

OK. Sorry. Goodbye.

Bye.

Step 3 Act out 2 dialogues with 2 different partners.

Around the year — Happy birthday

1 a) Listen and repeat.   ▶ Audio 77

winter	spring	summer	autumn
December January February	March April May	June July August	September October November

▶ Quiz
▶ AH S. 65 Nr. 1–2

b) Listen to the song. Stand up for your birthday month.   ▶ Audio 78–79

2 a) Listen to Noah and Finn.   ▶ Audio 80

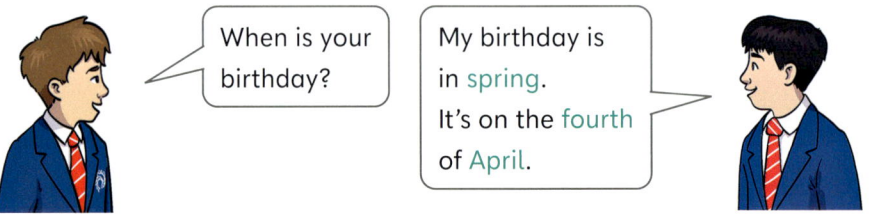

When is your birthday?

My birthday is in spring. It's on the fourth of April.

b) Listen and repeat.   ▶ Audio 81

MAY 1	MAY 2	MAY 3	MAY 4	MAY 25
first (1st)	second (2nd)	third (3rd)	fourth … (4th)	twenty-fifth (25th)

▶ Quiz
▶ AH S. 65 Nr. 3

c) Now you: Ask and answer.

When is your birthday?
- My birthday is in summer.
- It's on the ninth of July.

> Auf Seite 85 in diesem Buch findest du die **Ordnungszahlen** von 1. bis 31. In der **App** kannst du sie auch anhören.

▶ Numbers S. 85

66 sixty-six

3 a) Look and listen. Who is it?  Audio 82

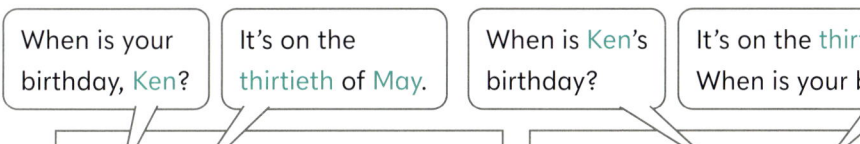

January	February	March	April
Amira 15th	Luca 20th	Rico 1st	Ella 3rd

b) Now you: Ask and answer in your class.

When is your birthday, Ken?

It's on the thirtieth of May.

When is Ken's birthday?

It's on the thirtieth of May. When is your birthday?

 Quiz

▶ AH S. 66 Nr. 1–2

4 a) Listen and read.  Audio 83

Happy birthday!

Have a cool party.

Happy birthday!

Have a great day.

A big birthday hug!

You are my best friend.

b) Write a birthday message. Save it and send it later.

▶ AH S. 66 Nr. 3

sixty-seven **67**

Happy Eid al-Fitr

1 Cartoon: Listen and read along.  Audio 84

2 Celebrations

> Mit dem **Zuckerfest** (Eid al-Fitr) endet im Islam die Fastenzeit (Ramadan). Viele Muslime und Musliminnen essen und trinken während der Fastenzeit tagsüber nichts. Am Zuckerfest essen und trinken alle wieder. Das Zuckerfest dauert meist drei Tage.
> Die Menschen besuchen Verwandte, Freunde und Nachbarn.
> Viele geben Spenden für arme Menschen. Die Kinder bekommen oft Süßigkeiten und Geschenke.
>
> - Was weißt du noch über das Zuckerfest?
> - Finde heraus: Wann ist Eid al-Fitr dieses Jahr?

▶ AH S. 67

Happy Hanukkah

1 a) Look and find ...
- the potato pancakes
- the donuts
- the presents
- the candles

b) Listen and say.  Audio 85
- When is Hanukkah?
- What food does Finn like?

2 a) Watch the video: How to make potato pancakes.  Video 10

b) Make potato pancakes.

3 Celebrations

Juden und Jüdinnen feiern **Chanukkah** (*Hanukkah*) im November oder Dezember. Das Lichterfest Chanukkah dauert acht Tage und Nächte. Man zündet jeden Abend eine Kerze an, bis alle Kerzen brennen. Viele Familien essen besondere Speisen. In manchen Familien bekommen die Kinder Geschenke.

- Was weißt du noch über Chanukkah?
- Finde heraus: Wann ist Chanukkah dieses Jahr?

▶ AH S. 68

sixty-nine **69**

Christmas and Boxing Day

1 Celebrations

In Großbritannien ist der 25. Dezember der Weihnachtstag.
Der 26. Dezember wird **Boxing Day** genannt. Früher hat man an diesem Tag Angestellten (z. B. dem Gärtner) ein Geschenk gegeben. Dieses Geschenk war in einer Schachtel (*box*).
Am 26. Dezember sind in Großbritannien die Geschäfte geöffnet. Viele Familien gehen einkaufen oder unternehmen etwas gemeinsam.

- Was machst du am 26. Dezember?
- Verschenkst du etwas zu Weihnachten?

2 Watch the video. Make a box.

▶ Video 11

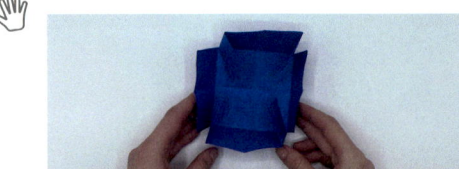

▶ AH S. 69 Nr. 1

3 a) Listen to Finn, Lily and Noah.

▶ Audio 86

What would you like for Christmas?

I'd like a new rucksack.

I'd like white sneakers.

b) Now you: Ask and answer.

What would you like for Christmas / your birthday / …?
– I'd like a rucksack / an orange rucksack.
– I'd like cool socks.

▶ Quiz
▶ AH S. 69 Nr. 2

New words and phrases

👁 💬 **Look and say.**

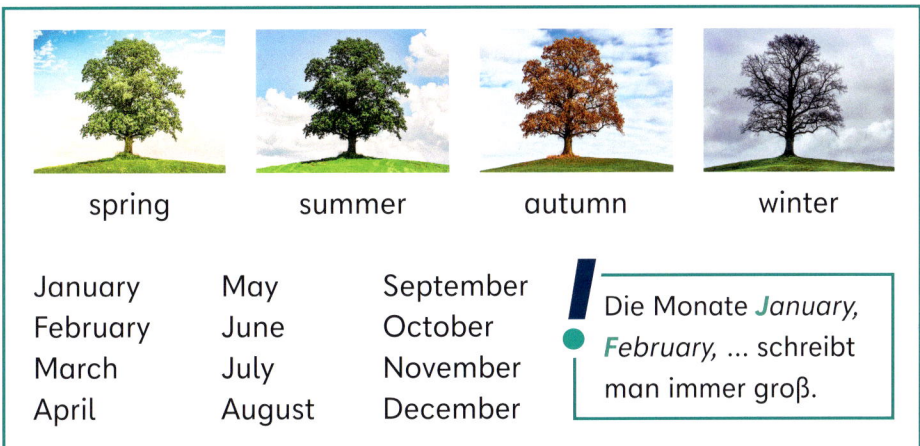

| spring | summer | autumn | winter |

January	May	September
February	June	October
March	July	November
April	August	December

❗ Die Monate *January*, *February*, ... schreibt man immer groß.

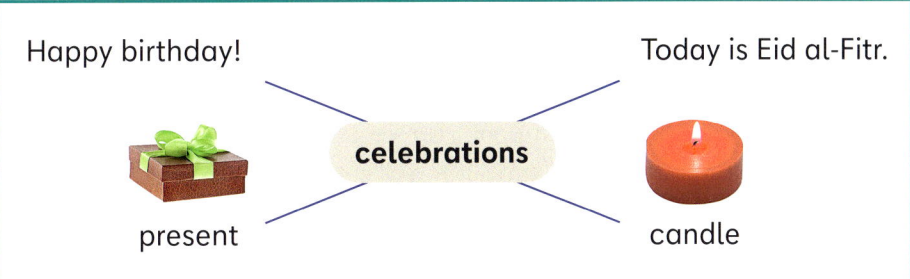

Happy birthday!   Today is Eid al-Fitr.

celebrations

present   candle

So sagst du, wann du Geburtstag hast und wann jemand anderes Geburtstag hat:

When is your birthday?
– My birthday is in summer.
– It's on the twenty-first of June.   *21st June*

When is Noah's birthday?
– It's on the thirtieth of May.   *30th May*

▶ Numbers S. 85

So sagst du, was du dir zum Geburtstag / ... wünschst:

What would you like for your birthday / ...?
– **I'd like** a new cap / an orange cap.
– **I'd like** cool socks.

❗ *I'd like* ist die Kurzform von *I would like*.

▶ AH S. 70

Hören mit dem Hör-Profi

Der Hör-Profi hilft mir, Hörtexte und Gespräche zu verstehen.
Ich merke mir die Schritte 1–3 des Hör-Profis. Ich wende den
Hör-Profi bei Hörtexten und Videos an.
Auf diesen Seiten kann ich üben: 7, 10, 11, 15, 18, 23, 26, 31, 34, 39,
50, 55, 58, 63, 66, 67, 69.

1 Vor dem Hören

Ich sehe mir die Bilder an.
Was sehe ich?
Was passiert?

Was kann ich auf Englisch sagen?

2 Beim Hören

OK, Lily. Let's start. Take out your book, …

Ich höre den Text einmal.
Welche Wörter verstehe ich?
Was sehe ich auch auf den Bildern?

> Bei Videos:
> Was sagen mir die Gesichter?
> Was tun die Hände?

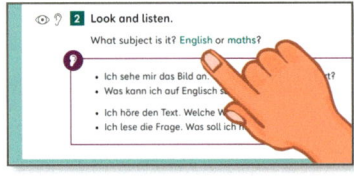

Ich lese die Fragen.
Worum geht es?
Was soll ich herausfinden?
Was verraten mir die Schlüsselwörter?

Ich höre den Text genau.
Was weiß ich jetzt?

3 Nach dem Hören

English

Ich beantworte die Fragen.

Ich überlege zum Schluss:
Was weiß ich jetzt?
Was habe ich gut gemacht?

Sprechen mit dem Sprech-Profi

Der Sprech-Profi hilft mir, deutlich und verständlich zu sprechen.
Ich merke mir die Schritte 1–3 des Sprech-Profis.
Ich wende den Sprech-Profi bei Sprech-Aufgaben an.
Auf diesen Seiten kann ich üben: 5, 6, 11, 12, 13, 19, 21, 25, 27, 28, 29, 33, 35, 41, 43, 45, 51, 57, 59, 61, 62, 65, 66, 67.

1 Vor dem Sprechen

Ich höre das Wort oder den Satz mehrmals.
Wie klingt das Wort?
Wie klingt der Satz?

Ich spreche leise mit.

2 Beim Sprechen

Ich spreche das Wort oder den Satz laut nach.
Wie klingt das bei mir?

Ich lese und sage das Wort oder den Satz.
Ich schließe die Augen und wiederhole laut.

Ich übe so lange, bis ich das Wort oder den Satz sicher sagen kann.

3 Nach dem Sprechen

Ich verwende das Wort oder den Satz so oft wie möglich.
Wo kann ich das Wort verwenden?
Wo kann ich den Satz verwenden?
Welche anderen Sätze kann ich genauso bilden?

Ich überlege zum Schluss:
Welche Wörter oder Sätze will ich mir merken?
Was habe ich gut gemacht?

Lesen mit dem Lese-Profi

Der Lese-Profi hilft mir, Texte zu lesen und zu verstehen.
Ich merke mir die Schritte 1–3 des Lese-Profis.
Ich wende den Lese-Profi bei Texten an.
Auf diesen Seiten kann ich üben: 14, 22, 30, 31, 38, 46, 47, 54, 62, 68.

1 Vor dem Lesen

Ich sehe mir die Bilder an.
Was sehe ich?
Was passiert?

2 Beim Lesen

Ich höre den Text und lese mit.
Welche Wörter verstehe ich?
Was sehe ich auch auf den Bildern?

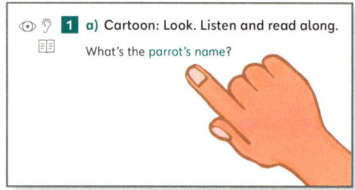

Ich lese die Fragen.
Was soll ich herausfinden?
Was verraten mir die Schlüsselwörter?

Ich lese den Text genau.
Ich achte auf die Schlüsselwörter.
Was weiß ich jetzt?

3 Nach dem Lesen

Ich beantworte die Fragen.

Ich überlege zum Schluss:
Was nehme ich aus dem Text mit?
Was habe ich gut gemacht?

Schreiben mit dem Schreib-Profi

Der Schreib-Profi hilft mir, richtig und verständlich zu schreiben.
Ich merke mir die Schritte 1–3 des Schreib-Profis.
Ich wende den Schreib-Profi an, wenn ich Wörter und Sätze schreibe.
Auf diesen Seiten kann ich üben: 12, 17, 37, 41, 49, 67.

1 Vor dem Schreiben

My friend has short brown hair.
My friend has green eyes.
My friend is helpful.
He is funny.
He is good at running.
We play football and we chill.

Ich sehe mir das Wort oder den Satz genau an.
Auf welche Buchstaben
muss ich besonders achten?

2 Beim Schreiben

Ich schreibe das Wort, den Satz sorgfältig ab.
Ich nutze die Hilfen in meinem Schulbuch:
Die blauen Wörter in den Sätzen sind Beispiele.
Ich ersetze diese blauen Wörter durch
meine eigenen Ideen.

3 Nach dem Schreiben

Ich überprüfe das Wort, Buchstabe für Buchstabe.
Ich überprüfe den ganzen Satz.
Habe ich alles richtig geschrieben?
Kann ich alles lesen und verstehen?

Wenn ich einen Fehler finde:
Ich verbessere das Wort oder den Satz.

My friend has long black hair.
My friend has brown eyes.
My frend is clever.
She is funi.

Wenn ich am PC schreibe,
erkenne ich Fehler an den
Wellenlinien unter den Wörtern.

Ich überlege zum Schluss:
Was kann ich jetzt?
Was habe ich gut gemacht?

seventy-five

Wörterliste

Wörter, die mit einem Kringel (°) markiert sind, gehören nicht zum Lernwortschatz.

A

a, an	ein, eine

Vor den Vokalen **a, e, i, o, u** *steht meist* **an**:

a banana	**an** apple
a melon	**an** orange
a new T-shirt	**an** old T-shirt

°activity	die Aktivität
and	und
animal	das Tier
ankle	der Knöchel, das Fußgelenk
apple	der Apfel
April	der April
are: The books are £2.	Die Bücher kosten 2 Pfund.
are: they are	sie sind
aren't: they aren't	sie sind nicht
arm	der Arm
art	die Kunst
at 8 o'clock	um 8 Uhr
at school	in der Schule
at the table	am Tisch
August	der August
aunt	die Tante
autumn	der Herbst

B

banana	die Banane
be	sein

Das Verb **be**:

I **am** (= I'm)	ich bin
you **are** (= you're)	du bist
he/she/it **is** (= he's/she's/it's)	er/sie/es ist
we **are** (= we're)	wir sind
you **are** (= you're)	ihr seid
they **are** (they're)	sie sind

°Be quiet.	Sei(d) leise.
beach	der Strand
bed	das Bett
°best friend	der beste Freund, die beste Freundin
big	groß
bike	das Fahrrad
birthday	der Geburtstag
black	schwarz
blond	blond
blue	blau
board	die Tafel
body	der Körper
book	das Buch
boring	langweilig
boy	der Junge
braces (Mehrzahl)	die Zahnspange, die Zahnklammer
bread	das Brot
breakfast	das Frühstück
brother	der Bruder
brown	braun
but	aber
butter	die Butter
Bye.	Tschüss.

C

°call	nennen; anrufen
can	können
candle	die Kerze
can't: I can't	ich kann nicht
cap	die (Schirm-)Mütze, die Kappe
card	die Karte
cash	das Bargeld
cat	die Katze
celebration	die Feier, das Fest
cereal	die Frühstücksflocken
chair	der Stuhl

cheese	der Käse
chicken	das Huhn; das Hähnchen
chill	chillen
chilling	das Chillen
chips *(Mehrzahl)*	die Pommes frites
cinema	das Kino
class	die Klasse; der Unterricht; der Kurs
clean	1. sauber 2. sauber machen, putzen
close	schließen, zumachen
clothes *(Mehrzahl)*	die Kleidung, die Kleidungsstücke
cold	kalt
colour	die Farbe
computer	der Computer
computer game	das Computerspiel
computing	die Informatik
cooking	das Kochen
cool	cool
corn	der Mais
cousin	der Cousin, die Cousine
cupboard	der Schrank
cushion	das Kissen
cycling	das Radfahren

D

dad	der Papa, der Vati
dancing	das Tanzen
day	der Tag
°**days of the week**	die Wochentage
December	der Dezember
desk	der Schreibtisch
dinner	das Abendessen
dirty	schmutzig
do homework	die Hausaufgaben machen

Do you like swimming?	Magst du Schwimmen?
do sport	Sport treiben
does: What does Lily eat?	Was isst Lily (gerne)?
doesn't: She doesn't eat …	Sie isst nicht …, Sie isst keine(n) …
Kurzformen und Langformen: doesn**'t** = does **not** don**'t** = do **not**	
dog	der Hund
door	die Tür
drawing	das Zeichnen
drink	1. das Getränk 2. trinken

E

eat	essen
egg	das Ei
eleven	elf
England	England
English	Englisch; englisch
every	jeder/jede/jedes
every Monday	jeden Montag
everybody	alle, jeder
exciting	aufregend
°**Excuse me, …**	Entschuldigung, …
exercise	die Übung, die Aufgabe
eye	das Auge

F

family	die Familie
father	der Vater
favourite	Lieblings-
February	der Februar
feel	fühlen; sich fühlen
film	der Film
finger	der Finger
first	erste(r, s)

Wörterliste

fish, *Mehrzahl:* **fish**	der Fisch
fit	passen
folder	die Mappe, der Ordner
food	das Essen, das Lebensmittel
foot, *Mehrzahl:* **feet**	der Fuß
football	der Fußball
for breakfast	zum Frühstück
for homework	als Hausaufgabe
fourth (4th)	vierte(r, s)
Friday	der Freitag
friend	der Freund, die Freundin
from	von, aus
°**fun**	der Spaß
funny	witzig, lustig

G

game	das Spiel
gaming	das Gaming *(das Spielen am Computer)*
gardening	das Gärtnern
German	Deutsch
Germany	Deutschland
°**Get well soon.**	Gute Besserung.
girl	das Mädchen
glasses *(Mehrzahl)*	die Brille
glue stick	der Klebestift
go	gehen; fahren
go shopping	einkaufen gehen
good	gut
good: be good at sth.	etwas gut können; gut in etwas sein
Good idea!	Gute Idee!
Good morning.	Guten Morgen.
Good to see you.	Schön, dich zu sehen.
Goodbye.	Auf Wiedersehen.
grandfather	der Großvater
grandma	die Oma
grandmother	die Großmutter
grandpa	der Opa
great	toll
green	grün
guinea pig	das Meerschweinchen

H

hair	das Haar, die Haare
ham	der Schinken
hamster	der Hamster
hand	die Hand
happy	glücklich, froh
Happy birthday!	Herzlichen Glückwunsch zum Geburtstag!
has: he/she/it has	er/sie/es hat
have	haben
he	er
head	der Kopf
Hello.	Hallo.
help	helfen
helpful	hilfsbereit; hilfreich
her name is	sie heißt
Here you are.	Bitte schön. / Hier, bitte.
Hi.	Hallo. Hi.
his name is	er heißt
history	die Geschichte *(das Schulfach)*
hobby, *Mehrzahl:* **hobbies**	das Hobby

> *Englisch:* hobb**y** – hobb**ies**
> *Deutsch:* das Hobb**y** – die Hobb**ys**

homework	die Hausaufgabe(n)

honest	ehrlich
horse	das Pferd
hot	heiß, warm
how	wie
How are you?	Wie geht's? / Wie geht es dir/euch?
How much is/are …?	Was (Wie viel) kostet/kosten …?
How old are you?	Wie alt bist du?
°hug	die Umarmung
hurt	wehtun

I

ice tea	der Eistee
idea	die Idee
I'm (= I am)	ich bin
I'm fine.	Mir geht es gut.
I'm sorry.	Tut mir leid.
in	in
in spring	im Frühling
°in the photo	auf dem Foto
°invitation	die Einladung
is	(er/sie/es) ist
is: The football is £3.	Der Fußball kostet 3 Pfund.
it	es
it's (= it is)	es ist (bei Sachen und Tieren auch: er ist; sie ist)

J

jacket	die Jacke, das Jackett
jam	die Marmelade
January	der Januar

Die Monate schreibt man immer groß:
January, **F**ebruary, **M**arch, …

jeans (Mehrzahl)	die Jeans

°job	der Job, die (Arbeits-) Stelle
juice	der Saft
July	der Juli
June	der Juni

K

°king	der König
knee	das Knie

Manche Buchstaben spricht man nicht aus:
knee („nii"), **h**onest („onest"), san**d**wich („sanwitsch"), **w**rite („rait"), …

L

lamp	die Lampe
leg	das Bein
lemonade	die Limonade
Let's …	Lass(t) uns …
like	mögen
lion	der Löwe
listen (to)	(sich etwas) anhören; zuhören
long	lang
look after my sister	auf meine Schwester aufpassen
loud	laut

M

make dinner	Abendessen machen
March	der März
maths	die Mathe(matik)
May	der Mai
meet	kennenlernen; (sich) treffen
°Mexican	mexikanisch
milk	die Milch

Wörterliste

Monday	der Montag

> Die Wochentage schreibt man immer groß:
> **M**onday, **T**uesday, **W**ednesday, …

monkey	der Affe
mother	die Mutter
mouse, Mehrzahl: **mice**	die Maus
Mr Lee	Herr Lee
Ms Bond	Frau Bond
mum	die Mama, die Mutti
mushroom	der Pilz, der Champignon
music	die Musik
°must	müssen

N

name	der Name
neighbour	der Nachbar, die Nachbarin
new	neu
next to	neben
nice	nett
Nice to meet you.	Schön, dich kennenzulernen.
no	nein
No, I don't. (freundliche Kurzantwort)	Nein.

> Auf die Frage **Do you like swimming?** solltest du nicht nur mit yes oder no antworten. Antworte mit **No, I don't.** oder **Yes, I do.** Das ist höflicher.

°No sports for two days.	Zwei Tage kein Sport.
not so	nicht so
November	der November
number	die Zahl, die Nummer

O

o'clock: 10 o'clock	10 Uhr
October	der Oktober
OK	OK, okay, in Ordnung
old	alt
on	auf
on Monday	am Montag
on the 4th of April	am vierten April
onion	die Zwiebel
open	1. öffnen; aufschlagen (Buch) °2. offen, geöffnet
°Open your books on page 10.	Schlagt eure Bücher auf Seite 10 auf.
°or	oder
orange	die Orange; orange(farben)
organizing	das Organisieren

P

page (= p.)	die (Buch-/Heft-)Seite
park	der Park
parrot	der Papagei
partner	der Partner, die Partnerin
party	die Party
pasta	die Pasta, die Nudeln
pay	zahlen, bezahlen
pay cash	bar bezahlen
pay by card	mit Karte bezahlen
pen	der Kugelschreiber, der Stift; der Füller
°pence	Mehrzahl von penny (kleinste britische Münze)
pencil	der Bleistift
pencil case	das Federmäppchen
pepper	die Paprika
pet	das (Haus-)Tier

phone	das Handy, das Telefon
°Pick a word.	Wähle ein Wort aus.
°picture	das Bild
pink	pink, rosa
pizza	die Pizza
place	der Ort, der Platz
play	spielen
playing	das Spielen
please	bitte
°potato pancake	der Kartoffelpuffer
pound (£)	das Pfund (britische Währung)

Man schreibt:	Man sagt:
£ 1	one **pound**
£ 2.50	two **pounds** fifty
90 p	ninety pence („pi")

present	das Geschenk

Q

°queen	die Königin
quiet	ruhig, still, leise

R

rabbit	das Kaninchen
rat	die Ratte
red	rot
°right: You are right.	Du hast Recht.
roll	das Brötchen
room	der Raum, das Zimmer
rubber	der/das Radiergummi
rucksack	der Rucksack
ruler	das Lineal
running	das Laufen, das Rennen

S

°sad	traurig
salad	der Salat *(als Gericht oder Beilage)*
sandwich	das Sandwich
Saturday	der Samstag, der Sonnabend
sausage	das Würstchen, die Wurst
°Say it again.	Sage es noch einmal.
school	die Schule
°school club	die AG (in der Schule)
school things	die Schulsachen
science	die Naturwissenschaft
second (2nd)	zweite(r, s)
see	sehen
September	der September
she	sie
shelf, *Mehrzahl:* **shelves**	das Regal(brett)
shoe	der Schuh
shop	das Geschäft, der Laden
shop assistant	der/die Verkäufer/in
shopping	das Einkaufen; die Einkäufe
short	kurz
shorts *(Mehrzahl)*	die kurze Hose, die Shorts
sick	krank
sister	die Schwester
sit	sitzen; sich setzen
skatepark	der Skatepark
skirt	der Rock
small	klein
snake	die Schlange
sock	die Socke
sofa	das Sofa

Wörterliste

some	einige, ein paar; etwas, ein wenig

> **Some** verwendet man
> 1. *wenn man etwas nicht zählen kann:*
>   **some** lemonade, **some** ice tea
> 2. *wenn man nicht weiß, wie viele es sind:*
>   **some** tomatoes

sport	der Sport; die Sportart
sports field	der Sportplatz, das Sportfeld
spring	der Frühling
°Stay at home for three days.	Bleibe drei Tage zuhause.
stomach	der Bauch
stressful	stressig
student	der Schüler, die Schülerin; der Student, die Studentin
subject	das (Schul-)Fach
summer	der Sommer
Sunday	der Sonntag
sweatshirt	das Sweatshirt
swimming	das Schwimmen
swimming pool	das Schwimmbad

T

table	1. der Tisch °2. die Tabelle
table tennis	das Tischtennis
takeaway	die Imbissbude; der Imbiss
tea	der Tee
teacher	der Lehrer, die Lehrerin
Tell me about …	Erzähle mir von …
thank you	danke (schön)
thanks	danke (schön)

°That's right.	Das ist richtig.
°That's wrong.	Das ist falsch.
the	der, die, das

> Den Artikel **the** spricht man verschieden aus:
> 1. *Vor Konsonanten wie „thä":*
>   **the ch**ips, **the h**am, **the p**izza
> 2. *Vor Vokalen meist wie „thi":*
>   **the i**ce tea, **the o**range, **the e**gg

there are	es gibt
there is	es gibt

> *So sagst du* „**Es gibt …**" *auf Englisch:*
> Einzahl: **There is** 1 chair.
> Mehrzahl: **There are** 2 chairs.
> Im Englischen spricht man den Laut „th" besonders aus. Höre dir folgende Wörter in einer Wörterbuch-App an: **th**anks, **th**ing, **th**ird und **th**e, **th**en, **th**ey.

they	sie *(Mehrzahl)*
third (3rd)	dritte(r, s)
thirteen	dreizehn (13)
°this	dieser, diese, dieses
This is Zane.	Das ist Zane.
Thursday	der Donnerstag
°time	die Zeit
tired	müde
to the board	an die Tafel
today	heute
°together	zusammen
tomato, *Mehrzahl:* **tomatoes**	die Tomate
too	auch
too small	zu klein
tooth, *Mehrzahl:* **teeth**	der Zahn
°touch	anfassen, berühren
°town	die Stadt
°trail running	der Geländelauf

trousers (Mehrzahl)	die Hose
Tuesday	der Dienstag
tuna	der Thunfisch
twenty-fifth (25th)	fünfundzwanzigste(r, s)

U

uncle	der Onkel
under	unter
°understand	verstehen
°uniform	die Uniform

V

veggie spread	der vegetarische Aufstrich
video	das Video

W

walk the dog	mit dem Hund spazieren gehen, Gassi gehen
wardrobe	der Kleiderschrank
watch	(sich etwas) anschauen
water	das Wasser
we	wir
Wednesday	der Mittwoch
°week	die Woche
Welcome (back)!	Willkommen (zurück)!
What about you?	Und du? / Was ist mit dir?
What would you like for Christmas?	Was wünschst du dir zu Weihnachten?
°What's missing?	Was fehlt?
What's your favourite animal?	Was ist dein Lieblingstier?
What's the time?	Wie spät ist es?
°What's this in English?	Wie heißt das auf Englisch?
What's your name?	Wie heißt du? (*wörtlich:* Was ist dein Name?)

What's ist die Kurzform von **What is**.

°When do … meet?	Wann treffen sich …?
When is your birthday?	Wann hast du Geburtstag?
Where …?	Wo …?
white	weiß
°who	wer
°Who is it?	Wer ist es?
window	das Fenster
winter	der Winter
with	mit
word	das Wort
work	arbeiten
Would you like …?	Möchtest du …?
would: I'd like … (= I would like)	Ich hätte gern …
write	schreiben

Y

°year	das Jahr; der Jahrgang
yellow	gelb
yes	ja
Yes, I do. (*freundliche Kurzantwort*)	Ja.
yoghurt	der/das Joghurt
you	du; dich; dir; ihr; euch; Sie; Ihnen
your	dein, deine
you're (= you are)	du bist; ihr seid; Sie sind
You're welcome.	Bitte, gern geschehen. / Nichts zu danken.
youth centre	das Jugendzentrum

Let's talk

Classroom English

You and your teacher	Du und dein Lehrer / deine Lehrerin
Good morning, Mr / Ms …	Guten Morgen, Herr / Frau …
Can I close / open the window, please?	Kann ich bitte das Fenster zumachen / aufmachen?
Can I go to the board?	Kann ich an die Tafel gehen?
Can we listen to a song?	Können wir ein Lied anhören?
Can we play a game?	Können wir ein Spiel spielen?
Goodbye.	Auf Wiedersehen.

You need help	Du brauchst Hilfe
Can you help me, please?	Können Sie mir bitte helfen? / Kannst du mir bitte helfen?
I don't understand.	Ich habe das nicht verstanden.
What's *Lineal* in English?	Was heißt „Lineal" auf Englisch?
What's „pen" in German?	Was heißt *pen* auf Deutsch?
What page, please?	Welche Seite, bitte?

Work with a partner	Zusammen arbeiten
Can I work with Kim?	Kann ich mit Kim arbeiten?
Can I have your pen, please?	Kann ich bitte deinen Stift haben?
Yes, here you are.	Ja. Hier, bitte.
Thanks, Tom.	Danke, Tom.

Give feedback	Feedback geben
Good work!	Gute Arbeit! Gut gemacht!
I like your poster / …	Mir gefällt dein Plakat / …
Your poster / … is cool.	Dein Plakat / … ist cool.
Your pictures are good.	Deine Bilder sind gut.

What your teacher says	Was dein Lehrer / deine Lehrerin sagt
Be quiet, please.	Sei bitte leise. / Seid bitte leise.
Do exercise 3 for homework.	Macht Übung 3 als Hausaufgabe.
Let's do exercise 3.	Lasst uns Übung 3 machen.
Listen, please.	Hör bitte zu. / Hört bitte zu.
Open your books on page 9.	Schlagt Seite 9 auf.
Say it again, please.	Sag das bitte noch mal.

Numbers

Du kannst dir die Grundzahlen 1 bis 100 in der App anhören.  Hilfe

1	one		20	twenty
2	two		21	twenty-one
3	three		22	twenty-two
4	four		23	twenty-three
5	five		24	twenty-four
6	six		25	twenty-five
7	seven		26	twenty-six
8	eight		27	twenty-seven
9	nine		28	twenty-eight
10	ten		29	twenty-nine
11	eleven		30	thirty
12	twelve		40	forty
13	thirteen		50	fifty
14	fourteen		60	sixty
15	fifteen		70	seventy
16	sixteen		80	eighty
17	seventeen		90	ninety
18	eighteen		100	one hundred / a hundred
19	nineteen			

Du kannst dir die Ordnungszahlen 1. bis 31. in der App anhören.  Hilfe

1st	first		17th	seventeenth
2nd	second		18th	eighteenth
3rd	third		19th	nineteenth
4th	fourth		20th	twentieth
5th	fifth		21st	twenty-first
6th	sixth		22nd	twenty-second
7th	seventh		23rd	twenty-third
8th	eighth		24th	twenty-fourth
9th	ninth		25th	twenty-fifth
10th	tenth		26th	twenty-sixth
11th	eleventh		27th	twenty-seventh
12th	twelfth		28th	twenty-eighth
13th	thirteenth		29th	twenty-ninth
14th	fourteenth		30th	thirtieth
15th	fifteenth		31st	thirty-first
16th	sixteenth			

Quellenverzeichnis

Titelbild
Cornelsen/Nils Fliegner

Illustrationen
Cornelsen/Inhouse/**Josephine Bienert-Köhler**: (S. 17, Step 1; S. 72–74; S. 75); Cornelsen/**Carl Pearce** (Beehive Illustration Agency): (S. 7 Nr. 5, S. 14 Nr. 1, S. 22 Nr. 1, S. 30 Nr. 1, S. 38, S. 46 Nr. 1, S. 54, S. 62); Cornelsen/**Joseph Wilkins** (Beehive Illustration Agency): (Umschlaginnenseite vorne [U2], S. 3 [4, 10, 18, 26, 34, 42, 58], S. 4–6, S. 7 Nr. 4 1–6, S. 8–16, S. 17 Step 2+ Step 3, S. 18–21, S. 22 Nr. 2, S. 24–29, S. 30 Nr. 2, S. 31 Nr. 3 oben li., oben re., S. 32, S. 33 oben re., Mi. li., Mi. re., S. 34–35, S. 36 Nr. 1a li., 1b, S. 37, S. 40, S. 41 unten li., unten re., S. 42–45, S. 48, S. 49 Step 2+Step 3, S. 50–53, S. 56, S. 57 Step 2+Step 3, S. 58–60, S. 61 Nr. 3, Nr. 4a, Nr. 5, S. 64, S. 65 Mi. li., Mi. re., S. 66 Nr. 2a, S. 67 Nr. 3a+b, S. 68, S. 69 Nr. 1 re., S. 70 unten, S. 84); Cornelsen/**Irina Zinner**: (Umschlaginnenseite hinten [U3]: Möwe)

Abbildungen
Cornelsen Lernen App-Seite: Handy-Rahmen: Shutterstock.com/Pavlo S, Tastatur: Shutterstock.com/Monory; S. 1 App-Symbol: Cornelsen/Inhouse/Anne Weingarten; S. 3 66: Shutterstock.com/elisekurenbina, 50: Shutterstock.com/Digital 2 Design; S. 14 Nr. 2: Shutterstock.com/Hintergrundbild: Komuso Colorsandia, Schild: GO DESIGN, Plastikhefter: LaMony Betty; S. 15 Nr. 3 1–3: Cornelsen/Anja Poehlmann, Delfine: Shutterstock.com; S. 23 Imago Stock & People GmbH/ZUMA Wire/LoredanaxSangiuliano; S. 31 Nr. 3 unten li.: Shutterstock.com/kstudija, Nr. 3 Mi.li.: Shutterstock.com/aarrows, Nr. 3 Mi.re.: Shutterstock.com/YanzStudio, Nr. 3 unten re.: Shutterstock.com/AstworkStudio; S. 33 oben li.: Cornelsen / ©Duden Learnattack GmbH – www.dudenlearnattack.de; S. 36 Nr. 1 re.: Cornelsen/Anja Poehlmann; S. 39 unten re.: mauritius images/alamy stock photo/Scott Hortop Travel, oben li.: mauritius images/alamy stock photo/Rob Carter, oben re.: mauritius images/Loop Images, unten li.: Shutterstock.com/Jakov Simovic; S. 41 oben li.: Cornelsen / ©Duden Learnattack GmbH – www.dudenlearnattack.de; S. 46 unten re.: Shutterstock.com/Indian Food Images; unten li.: Shutterstock.com/StockImageFactory.com; S. 47 unten re.: Shutterstock.com/stocksolutions, Rind, Huhn, Karotte: Shutterstock.com/Giraphics, Burger: Shutterstock.com/Graphic GT, Fish and chips: Shutterstock.com/LplusD, Flaschen Icon: Shutterstock.com/Imagination lol, Pizza: Shutterstock.com/Sabelskaya, Chillis: Shutterstock.com/Sudowoodo; S. 49 oben li.: Shutterstock.com/Valenty; S. 55 Emojis: Shutterstock.com/SpicyTruffel, Mi. re.: Shutterstock.com/ESB Professional; S. 57 oben li.: Cornelsen / ©Duden Learnattack GmbH – www.dudenlearnattack.de; S. 61 Nr. 4b: Shutterstock.com/gomolach; S. 63 10 pounds, 20 pounds, 50 pounds: Imago Stock & People GmbH/Cover-Images, 5 pounds: Imago Stock & People GmbH/AAP, pence (coins): © 2023 The Royal Mint Limited, Nr. 4 Cornelsen/alle Shutterstock.com/oben: timages, re.: Paul Maguire, unten: Mike Taylor, li.: Claudio Divizia; S. 65 oben li.: Cornelsen / ©Duden Learnattack GmbH – www.dudenlearnattack.de; S. 66 Nr. 1a: Shutterstock.com/by-studio, Nr. 2b: Shutterstock.com/Kanate; S. 67 unten Mi.: Shutterstock.com/Nika Karpenko, unten li.: Shutterstock.com/SHD Design, unten re.: Shutterstock.com/ArtMela, Geschenk: Shutterstock.com/elisekurenbina; S. 69 Geschenke, Kerzen: Shutterstock.com/ArnaPhoto, Mi. li. und Mi. re.: Cornelsen / ©Duden Learnattack GmbH – www.dudenlearnattack.de; unten re.: Shutterstock.com/Inna Reznik; S. 70 oben re.: Shutterstock.com/elisekurenbina, Mi.: Cornelsen / ©Duden Learnattack GmbH – www.dudenlearnattack.de; S. 71 Bäume: Shutterstock.com/by-studio, Mi. li.: Shutterstock.com/Madlen, Mi. re.: Shutterstock.com/Mister Tvister; S. 81 Shutterstock.com/Filatova Halyna; Umschlaginnenseite hinten (U3): Karte: stock.adobe.com/lesniewski

Liedquelle
S. 55 *Friday I'm in Love* by The Cure; BMG Music Publishing Ltd. / Musik Edition Discoton GmbH, Berlin. Text: Simon Johnathon Gallup / Perry Bamonte / Robert James Smith / Porl Thompson / Boris Williams